All About Collecting
Boys' Series Books

Hardy Boys®
Tom Swift®
Tom Swift, Jr.
Chip Hilton
Ted Scott
Mark Tidd
Tom Slade
& Others

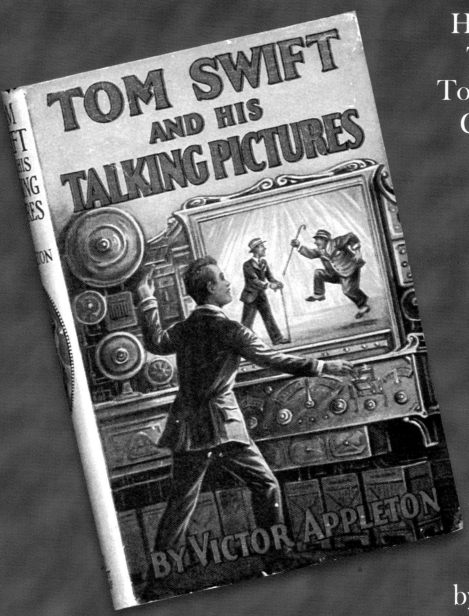

by John Axe

 Published by   Hobby House Press, Inc.
Hobby House Press   Grantsville, Maryland
www.hobbyhouse.com

Dedication

To Frank and Joe

Acknowledgments

I am very lucky to have the help and cooperation of friends and professionals in doing projects such as this one.

I appreciate everyone at Hobby House Press, Inc., particularly Gary R. Ruddell, Virginia Ann Heyerdahl, Brenda Wiseman, Theresa Black, and Sherry White.

I am grateful to my friends and fellow collectors, especially Linda Burns, Phyllis Butters, James D. Keeline, Sharon Kissell, Garrett K. Lothe, Gil O'Gara, Marge Meisinger, Jerry Olson, Lorraine Rogers, Jim Towey, and Karen Waterlander.

And I thank Donna Mehalco, Branch Manager, and Theresa Thompson, Operations Assistant, at ComDoc, who made my job easier and more enjoyable.

Additional copies of this book may be purchased at $27.95 (plus postage and handling) from

Hobby House Press, Inc.
1 Corporate Drive, Grantsville, MD 21536
1-800-554-1447
www.hobbyhouse.com
or from your favorite bookstore or dealer.

©2002 by John Axe

All rights reserved. No part of this book may be reproduced or utilized in any form or by any means, electronic or mechanical, including photocopying, recording, or by an information storage and retrieval system, without permission in writing from the publisher. Inquiries should be addressed to Hobby House Press, Inc., 1 Corporate Drive, Grantsville, MD 21536.

Printed in the United States of America

ISBN: 0-87588-636-1

Table of Contents

Foreword

I developed my interest in series books at the same time I learned that there were books written for children. The year that I began grade school I got *The Bobbsey Twins on a Houseboat* for Christmas. The dust jacket told that there were more books in the series and I wanted them. Bobbsey Twins books were what I wanted for birthday and Christmas presents the next few years. Thanks to Montgomery Ward's catalog, I learned about the existence of other books that appealed to me then and many of them were series books. I saved my allowance and any other money I got and placed an order with Montgomery Ward.

The first book I ordered was *Heidi's Children*. I think that it cost 65 cents and 10 cents for postage. I still have this book, as well as every other book I ever had as a child and they all have their dust jackets and are in very good condition. This was more than fifty years ago.

Like many collectors of their childhood memorabilia, I did not concentrate much on my series books for a long time but for several years now I have come back to them with the same passion I had fifty years ago. In the meantime I bought series books at flea markets, books sales and other places, if they were a bargain, and put them away. I now wish I had done more of that. The books I liked as a child were Judy Bolton, Nancy Drew®, the Hardy Boys®, the Five Little Peppers, the Albert Payson Terhune series of dog stories, and the Louisa May Alcott books. I also have many volumes of other series, but I never tried to complete the sets, or else I was not able to.

The money for my books came from my allowance, birthday gifts, and what I earned. When I was about eight years old I got a job during the school year washing blackboards for Miss Adams who gave me a quarter a week for this. Soon Mrs. Moore had me do her boards also and right after that Mrs. Fruit, in the room next to her, did the same. What I earned from these high school teachers came out to a book a week, as most series books cost 75 cents each then. By 1951, the Grosset & Dunlap books were 85 cents and before long they were 95 cents each, but by that time I had a paper route, which paid more than blackboard washing did.

Sometime in 1949, while we were playing in the basement of my cousin's house, I came across *The Mystery of the Ivory Charm*, an old thick Nancy Drew® book with orange endpapers. I was told that I could have it when I wanted to borrow it. To me, Nancy Drew® was "adult" reading matter and very exciting because of the cliffhangers at the end of each chapter. That Christmas my "Want List" included Nancy Drew® books, and I got *The Clue of the Leaning Chimney* and *The Mystery of the Tolling Bell*. This resulted in an addiction that did not end until I had the entire set of Nancy Drew® books.

In Sunday School, I told my friend Donna about Nancy Drew®. She insisted that there was a better series to read and loaned me the first Judy Bolton book, *The Vanishing Shadow*. This mystery was so advanced for me at that age that I did not fully understand all the plot nuances, but again I became addicted and acquired the whole set of Judy Bolton books. For Christmas of 1951 alone I received four of this set from three different people.

Although I spent all the money I could get on books, each one of them was very important to me. I purchased dozens of series books (and others) in the early 1950s. I can remember where I acquired most of them and even where they were located on the shelf in the store. By that time, I had found several stores that carried series books. Back then small department stores and stationery shops had a small selection of series books that they stocked for Christmas. I was their best customer on a yearly basis. My favorite place to buy books was a toyshop of a kind that no longer exists. This store carried a better line of toys than such places as G.C. Murphy and Woolworth's. During the Christmas season, its front window was full of the latest Madame Alexander dolls, which was about the only place in the store where there was much of a display. This was the old-fashioned sort of long, narrow store with an unpainted wooden floor and most things were kept in boxes up on shelves or in drawers. The back half of the store was for wallpaper and paint, probably the merchandise that made the store profitable. In between these two sections was a large square bookcase with series books on all four sides. They were arranged in shelves from near the floor to above my eye level. At that time merchandise was presented to the customer after it was paid for differently than it is today. A book was wrapped in heavy brown paper and carefully tied up with string instead of being casually dropped into a bag.

The book I bought there was *The Password to Larkspur Lane*, the first Nancy Drew® I purchased. This was in January 1950. I pulled out each of the Nancy Drew® books and studied them and picked this one because of the picture on the dust jacket. The dramatic scene on the cover of the book shows Nancy kneeling at a high wire fence; an old lady in a wheelchair is on the other side. A mean-looking man is coming toward them from a mansion in the background and the old lady is cautioning Nancy to remain silent. This is the sort of picture that tells that something exciting and dangerous is about to happen. I eventually had the whole set of Nancy Drew® books, but each one that I bought was because the picture on the cover made me want it, based on what I had come to expect from the mystery stories in the series.

This is not a unique situation. I have friends who also bought their books after carefully examining all the pictures on the covers of the ones available at the time. Janet went for *The Clue in the Old Album*, which she considers has the most beautiful Nancy Drew® dust jacket picture. She can also remember where the book was on the shelf in the store and, like me, can remember what shop each one came from although there are many. I am lucky that I still have all my books, as well as the memories associated with them. I can remember where I was when I read a certain book, what the weather was like that day and what was going on at home during the time I was reading it. Naturally I kept a list of the books I read and I gave each one a rating. All these details that we remember show the importance of series books in our lives.

I had another friend who later became a major league baseball player and a rookie of the year.

Needless to mention, he did not think much of Nancy Drew® and Judy Bolton and introduced me to the Hardy Boys®. I did not find this series as "adult" as Judy Bolton but the adventures of Frank and Joe were more thrilling than any I had read. The Hardy Boys® books were the only series books the local library had so I went through them and bought more of the set.

By the time I was about eleven years old I had written a couple of books myself, including some about two teenage brothers who solved mysteries and had dangerous adventures. One volume told about the time they drove their car across Lake Erie in the winter when it was frozen to pursue thieves in Canada. Far out in the lake, where the ice was not as solid, it broke up and the car went under; the boys (let's call them Frank and Joe) were rescued. At least my plot was original.

When I was young I also read the Tom Sawyer books and some of the Horatio Alger books. These were somewhat interesting, but no books appealed to me as much as the ones I considered contemporary, such as the Hardy Boys® series, although many of them had been written long before I was born. I imagine that I identified more with boys who drove motorcycles and cars than I did with ones who rafted on the Mississippi River or sold newspapers in New York City.

People who do not collect books wonder why we do. I am always amazed when somebody comes into my house, sees all the books and (always) asks, "Have you read all those books?" I remember a summer day when I was about three years old. I was lying on the grass with a Bible that I had asked for after I saw them in Sunday School. I studied the printed page and thought that I could read it; of course I couldn't. I finally did learn to read before I went to first grade in a one-room country school. One afternoon, when I was in first grade, the teacher began reading *Beautiful Joe* to the students because everyone was upset after Frances Thompson's mother came to the school to let us know that Frances died the night before. The beginning of this book is certainly far from uplifting, but I really liked Frances and it did distract me. And I learned a lot of new things by listening to the teacher reading *Beautiful Joe* and by reading many more books myself, up to the point where I taught History in a university, based a great deal on things that I had read.

Now the series books that interest me cost more than 65 cents each, although considering inflation I have "found" books that cost even less. I am as passionate about them as I was more than fifty years ago. There are also more places to acquire them now than there was back then.

Everyone I know who collects things likes to brag about their important finds and bargains. This is part of the excitement that collecting causes and also helps to justify the enormous quantities that we can acquire.

Of course there are used books stores and sales lists from which to purchase old series books. The bargains are usually not going to be on book dealers' lists. It is still possible to find a huge bargain in a used books shop. Just recently I got one of the last Tom Swift® Jr. books in one in Concord, Massachusetts, for $1, along with many other volumes in the same series that would be graded "Very Good." Sometimes a book may seem high priced on a list of books for sale, but if it is one that is needed to help fill out a series or has been a "Want" for a long time the unexpected cost for it can be justified.

There are also antiquarian book fairs where knowledgeable dealers sell series books. There are not always the same sort of bargains that can be found at even a used books shop at these shows, but usually books are sold at a fair price, or even lower than expected, and discounts may be given. Book fairs are also excellent for making contacts with whom to leave "Want Lists."

Antique shops and antique malls are excellent sources for old series books. I have found white spine Hardy Boys® books for $5 very recently. A couple of years ago I found a "blank ends" Nancy Drew® for $10, which is a tiny fraction of its current worth. It can also go the other way: A Nancy Drew® or Hardy Boys® picture cover book in horrible shape can be priced at $20 or more. One just laughs and goes on. My best bargains in recent years have come from antique shops or antique malls, but of course one has to visit many, many of them to find series book bargains.

Now we also have a whole world supply of books that did not exist just a few years ago. These are Internet auctions and sellers, such as eBay and Amazon.com. Just a few years ago when I first got a computer I finished off sets of series books with elusive volumes I had been hunting for more than forty years, all within a six-month period. The prices were not bad for most of these books. Some were many, many dollars more than I ever expected to pay. Another good source of series books is on-line sales lists. These are on such sources as "abebooks.com," and are offered for sale by knowledgeable professionals, which is not to say that they charge too much. Many times I have seen the same book for sale at less than half what the bids for it are bringing on eBay.

Some collectors find great series books for tremendous bargain prices at yard sales. Even thrift shops and charity outlets can be sources for finds.

The end result of a search at any of the above is often the most exciting part of collecting series books.

Sears and Roebuck and Co. Catalog, Fall and Winter 1930-1. Note that the books are priced "Postpaid" for 46 cents each. At the time the retail price of these books was 50 cents in stores. In 1930 there were already nine Hardy Boys® books, yet the emphasis here is on Tom Swift® and Ted Scott. *Marge Meisinger Collection.*

6

Chapter 1

Introduction

Values

I admit that value guides for any collectible item are not necessarily good things. However, they can be useful things. If something is worth collecting it is worth conserving and hence it has a value.

Price guides usually carry the disclaimer "The prices are guides; they are not absolutes" or something similar. It is the purpose of this book to show many of the most popular boys' series books that are collected in large numbers and to establish retail prices for them. The author recognizes the fact that when prices are established for any collectible, with a book they can cause those who do not understand the product or its value to place a price on it that has little bearing with reality. In other words, it can cause prices to rise. But on the other hand, if this is the case, it can also cause the value of something already owned in a collection to escalate in worth.

The price ranges given for series books in this volume have a very wide difference between the lowest price and the highest price. This is because **condition is everything in pricing a used book.** Rarity is also an important factor, so this is reflected in the price. In general, **a series book without a dust jacket is worth only a fraction of the same one with a dust jacket**. And the better the condition of the dust jacket, the more the book is worth. Example:

The Hardy Boys®, The Crisscross Shadow
Format V (1950s) – **$5.00-$45.00**

This means that a book in poor condition without a dust jacket is valued at $5; one in fine condition with an excellent dust jacket is valued at $45. That is to say, the range is from the worst book of the format to the best example. Books that are in horrible condition are not considered, as they have no value. "First Printings" are taken into consideration by the fact that they are "Format I" or are the high value.

Nothing is going to prevent a person who does not understand old books, let alone series books, from listing them for sale as this: "Wonderful old example of Heidi book, probably first edition, a must for any Heidi collector. Cover loose and torn, ink marks, the first few pages missing, but very good for its age. Only $19.95." The book is actually about five years old and has no value for a collector and should be priced at under a dollar. But don't bother to inform the seller of this, because he doesn't want to know it. He is not seeking knowledge or information; he is seeking a sale. Information would only offend him. Make your statement by ignoring the book.

The prices given in this book are those that are currently asked for books by knowledgeable book dealers and collectors. The Internet and eBay are taken into consideration. Anyone can ask any price they choose to; anyone can pay any price they want to.

In the past, collectors of old books who were seeking to add to their collections depended on book dealers; dealers "lists;" advertisements in magazines, newsletters and journals; antiquarian book shows; antique shops; flea markets; auctions; and other sources. This is the slow way to add to a collection. Now a collection can be completed more quickly with Internet listings and auctions on the Internet. How long would it take a person searching for Hardy Boys® books or Judy Bolton books to locate and look at 966 books using the older, more traditional methods? On March 6, 2002, to be exact, there were 966 Hardy Boys® books up for auction on eBay. There were also more copies available through computer listings of books for sale. Computers and the Internet are not for everybody, but this method of collecting is much more efficient, although nothing will ever replace the search at a book sale or the excitement of seeing one a collector "needs" and can pick up and hold in a shop even before paying for it.

It is true that many prices on eBay auctions are high because two or three people are desperate to have a certain book that day and the next time the same title is up for auction the price may be lower. Or it may be even higher because collectors have seen how much people are willing to pay for it. But bargains can be found even on eBay and not every auction ends up with a "sniper" grabbing it in the last thirty seconds for 50 cents more than you have been bidding for a week.

I have gathered my prices from all of the above sources and from my own evaluation and judgment, having collected series books most of my life.

Most old books and collectible books are sold through "lists" and through mail order. Because of this, accurate wording and descriptions must be used if both the seller and the buyer are to understand the condition of the book. The following guide for grading books is taken from *AB Bookman's Weekly,* which has been using this reference since 1949. It should be used as the standard for all buyers and sellers of old books.

As New The book looks perfect, as it did when first published.

Fine The book is close to "as new," but is not totally crisp.

Very Good Some signs of wear are present, such as a crease or a tiny tear (called a chip) in the dust jacket. Defects must be noted.

Good The book and dust jacket show minor wear but defects are not too distracting. All imperfections must be noted.

Fair This is a worn book and/or dust jacket that is complete and acceptable if described properly, with all defects noted.

Poor This is a badly worn book, called a "reading copy." It is not worth anything as a collectible.

The abbreviations for the above are: **FN, VG, GD, FR, PR**.

Two other conditions must be noted in old books: **Ex-libris** means that the book was a library book and has evidence of this with stamped information or card pockets. **Book Club Editions**, no matter what their condition, should always be noted. Collectors usually scorn these two designations unless the book is very rare and difficult to locate in better condition or in a standard printing.

The lack of a dust jacket must also be noted. It is standard procedure to rate both the dust jacket and the book, with the dust jacket rating listed first. An example of a description would be: "GD/GD. Minor chipping to DJ [dust jacket] spine top and bottom; slightly cocked spine; minor foxing on page ends."

Cleaning Collectible Books

Some museum curators consider the dirt that is in many artifacts to be part of their originality and do not remove it. An example is the dust and dirt found in Navaho and other Native American rugs and blankets. Other curators realize that dirt causes deterioration and also attracts microscopic pests that, in time, destroy things made of paper, such as books.

I always clean the books I buy because it probably does prolong their lives and it certainly makes them look much better. It can also improve their smell. The following is how I clean my books, based on years of experience in doing this.

First, remove the dust jacket and clean the book itself. Spray some commercial glass cleaner on a paper towel and carefully wipe off the covers of the book. Be careful with this, as the coloring agent in some cloth covers will run or rub off. Never spray a cleaner directly onto the book. Next, clean all the page edges, especially the top edges. Do this carefully with a soft, kneaded eraser, never with a pencil eraser or other hard eraser. Hold the pages tightly together when running the kneaded eraser over them to prevent bending or tearing.

The next process is to microwave the book. This will kill the fungus that causes mildew, which leaves spots, marks and an odor. Fan the pages of the book out and set it in the center of the microwave. Microwave on high for five seconds. Check the book. If there is no problem caused by microwaving it, give it another five seconds. In time, if the book is placed where it is in contact with fresh air, the smell from the mildew will be minimized. I have done this to books that were kept in a damp environment for about thirty years and now they no longer have an objectionable odor. Another positive result of this technique is it eliminates the factors that give allergic reactions to some people. (I sometimes set the microwave at longer lengths of time than ten seconds, based on my experience on how much time a book can endure without experiencing damage.)

If the book has any bent or folded pages and corners, straighten them and iron them. Use a regular iron on a high or hot setting. Cover each bend to be ironed with a sheet of paper toweling before ironing it. With some practice, one will also be able to determine how much ironing a page can withstand without the protection of the paper towel. It is also possible to remove some crease marks completely by dampening the spot before ironing, but proceed with caution. Do it with minimal water several times rather than allowing the page to become too wet all at once.

Erase any pencil marks inside the book with a kneaded eraser. Never use a pencil eraser, as this causes lifting and roughening of the page. Do not remove inscriptions, such as "To Dickie on his 10th Birthday. Love, Grandma, July 14, 1936," as this gives an old book charm as well as establishes when it was presumably new and is part of its historical provenance. If the original price from a store, or the price that a book dealer put in the book is in evidence, leave it, because it is also part of a book's history.

The most valuable part of an old series book is its dust jacket, so special attention is required to preserve it. Most dust jackets were originally varnished to protect them, either entirely or over the front cover picture only. Almost all Grosset & Dunlap books have only the picture varnished, with about 1/8 inch of varnish extended on both sides of the picture. I point this out because the varnished part of the dust jacket can be cleaned more vigorously than the rest of the paper covering, and it is usually the most soiled portion.

To clean a really dirty and stained dust jacket, lay it flat on a smooth surface and wipe it off with a paper towel that has been dampened with window cleaner. Do not use

Sears Christmas Book, 1944. In 1944 Sears' books for boys featured war pilot stories. The books were "Postpaid" at 58 cents each. At this time titles cost 60 cents in stores. *Marge Meisinger Collection.*

too much abrasion or too much fluid, as it can affect the ink on the dust jacket, as well as remove the varnish over the front picture, giving it a streaky effect. Be especially careful of those that are done with red or blue ink as this will wipe off. For an average cleaning job, the best thing to wipe a dust jacket off with is cigarette lighter fluid. Naturally safety precautions must be taken, but the lighter fluid will not discolor or harm the paper in any way, even if it is soaked with it. Another good cleaner for dust jackets (and for picture cover books) is Turtle Wax® Zip Wax®. However, only use this cleaner over a varnished dust jacket.

Many dust jackets have a worse enemy than dirt: tape and price stickers. If the price sticker is an original book price, never remove it. If masking tape or a price sticker is on the jacket from a yard sale, for example, this should be removed. Very carefully. Never, never pull a pressure sticker off a dust jacket, no matter how careful you are, as it almost always causes lifting of the picture surface. Most stickers and tape will loosen enough to remove them cautiously if the area is well heated with a hair dryer. Some transparent tape will also come off this way. To remove the sticky residue left from tape, wipe the area with a paper towel that has been dipped in vegetable oil. (Be very frugal with applying vegetable oil to paper; use it only on non-absorbent paper, such as a varnished dust jacket.) All transparent tape should be removed, as this will discolor the paper in time and spoil the dust jacket. Easier said than done. If the tape will not lift off after it has been heated with a hair dryer or soaked with cigarette lighter fluid, it has to stay on.

The next stage in reviving an old book is to iron the clean dust jacket. Lay the dust jacket flat on a hard, smooth surface, such as a kitchen counter, and iron it with a reasonably hot iron, placing a piece of paper towel between the iron and the dust jacket. Never iron directly on the dust jacket, as it will pucker up and the iron may

stick to it. This ironing process is especially important for dust jackets on books that have been lying flat with other books piled on top of them, causing the paper from the dust jacket to conform to the contours of the book and to become weak from pressure.

Minor tears or "chips" on a dust jacket should be left alone. If a tear is major or if the dust jacket is in danger of separating into two or more pieces, it should be mended. The tear should never be closed with transparent tape or any other tape (unless one uses professional, non-acidic book tape), as it stains the paper of the dust jacket and becomes brittle with time. The method I use to close tears is to cut strips of acid-free paper about the width of a piece of transparent tape, or wider if necessary, and apply them with glue from a glue stick (on the back side, or course). This is using the restoration method of not applying anything that could not be safely removed again.

The final stage in preservation and protection is to cover the dust jacket with an acid-free polyester cover. These cost about $1 per book if purchased separately. If a collector has many books to cover it is more cost-effective to order a roll of this material. Look on the back of one of these covers to see the name and address of the distributor and call him directly. For about $40 a roll, one can do about 300 books. The scraps of paper backing left over from the cover are perfect for making mending strips for dust jackets, as they are acid-free.

After all this restoration and preparation, use common sense in shelving and displaying books. Never let direct sunlight fall on the spines of books, as this will fade them almost "overnight." Do not pile books up or put things on top of them when they are shelved as this will cause stress and damage the spines. Keep books out of a damp or humid environment, as this is one of their worst enemies. With minimal precaution, your books will last longer than you.

Boys' Series Books are book sets in which more than one volume is about the same characters and the stories are meant to appeal primarily to young boys, or young men, of about ten to fifteen years old. The sets contain anywhere from two volumes to well over one hundred volumes.

Series books for juveniles owe part of their origin to the "dime novels" of the late 19th century. These short, cheaply produced books were meant for popular adult entertainment and were adventure stories and detective stories. Another antecedent of the popular Series Books of the 20th century was the "rags to riches" books for boys by Horatio Alger. Alger wrote dozens of volumes of books about poor boys who rose to success through hard work and belief in American ideals. The first was *Ragged Dick, or Life on the Streets* in 1867. This tale was so successful that Alger spent the rest of his life duplicating the pattern, which was enormously popular for the rest of the century and well into the 20th century. The "Alger hero" became an American literary term.

Edward Stratemeyer deserves the credit he gets for inventing the modern concept of juvenile series fiction, beginning with all the books he wrote for boys starting in the last part of the 19th century and which continues today with the Hardy Boys® and Nancy Drew® series. (See Chapter II, **Edward Stratemeyer.**) The early Stratemeyer Syndicate books concentrated on reading material for boys but in 1868, thirty years before his first big success, *Under Dewey at Manila*, was published in 1898, Louisa May Alcott's first volume in the *Little Women* series was released. In some ways, the Stratemeyer and Alcott books seem xenophobic, racist, offensive and anachronistic today, but they must be judged against the standards of their own times rather than against contemporary values.

One of the most important ways in which anyone can acquire an education is to read books. All sorts of books have been written and people have learned many things from them. Not all books have been deliberately written for educational purposes and one of the most important types of books has always been what is known as "literature," such as the novel or epic. These books can inform readers of history, culture, religion, values, ethics, standards of conduct, and many other good things. The chief function of the novel has always been to entertain though. In its day, storytellers and singers repeated Homer's *Iliad* to entertain the public. Series books were written to entertain young people, just as were the works of Mark Twain and James Fenimore Cooper, whom librarians held in higher esteem, although one can learn important things from all of them.

Towards the end of the 19th century and the beginning of the 20th century the trend for juvenile series books developed strongly, as they could be produced more economically than before that time. Many books written primarily for boys, such as Edgar Rice Burroughs' *Tarzan* and early Stratemeyer books written under names such as Arthur M. Winfield (thirty Rover Boys books), Clarence Young (twenty-two Motor Boys books), and Victor Appleton (forty Tom Swift® books) sold very well. All these series books were exciting, fast-paced, adventurous, and very entertaining and they became the standard for all other writers to imitate if they also wanted to be successful. Collectors of series books today are fortunate indeed that libraries did not shelf many boys' series books. They were well liked in spite of this lack of validation by professionals and so they had to be purchased, as they were not available for free. The fact that huge quantities of series books were published and sold has allowed for their continuing existence for collectors today.

There were scores of boys' series books available all during the 20th century from several different publishers. The most popular ones were from Grosset & Dunlap and many of these were Stratemeyer books, such as the Radio Boys, Don Sturdy, the X Bar X Boys, Ted Scott, and Tom Swift®, Jr. The most important non-Stratemeyer series for Grosset & Dunlap were the Leo Edwards books, Chip Hilton and Rick Brant. Cupples & Leon gave us Bomba, the Jungle Boy, another Stratemeyer product. Harper and Brothers had Clarence Budington Kelland's Catty Atkins and Mark Tidd.

In time, the most important boys' series books, and the ones that are the most highly sought and collected today, involved young detectives, such as the Hardy Boys®. This way the story can combine romance, adventure and mystery, offering as many popular fiction or novel genres in one volume as possible.

It is commonly believed that series books are not popular nor are they available for today's youth. This is not true at all. The books stores in the malls are full of them. True, they are not the quality products of the 1930s, but they are there in great abundance in paperback form, especially the new Hardy Boys® books. They are already collectible.

The classic boys' series sets began to decline with the paper shortages of the World War II era, and more importantly with changes in public (including juvenile) taste in the years following World War II, although there now are undoubtedly more books sold to juveniles than ever before in history. The newer series books do not seem to have the permanent importance they did in the past, but that is for another generation of readers to decide in the future.

What is it that makes certain boys' series books so desirable as collectibles today? One factor is that they have to have been appreciated by both girls and boys. (How many people collect Little Colonel books?) And this means that both women and men collect them at the present time. They have to have some universal quality of acceptance about them to be still so desirable. Remember, series books are not collected only for display purposes. They can also be read! And enjoyed. (It would be interesting to know the ratio of boys who also read Nancy Drew® and girls who also read the Hardy Boys®.) The heroes of boys' series books have to be someone that the authors created as likable personalities whose qualities endure for many generations. The books also have to be ones that adults can still enjoy. Few adults read the Stratemeyer Bobbsey Twins books or the Buddy books and the Curlytops by Howard R. Garis, as they were written for very young children.

Those who collect Tom Swift® books, for example, read them over and over. It is quite certain that those who do so, enjoy reading the books and remembering the plot devices and surprises in the stories. Some of these people are "buffs" who know the story better than the author would. They are also reliving their youth and a time when everything was new and the future was full of promise. It is probably true that older people enjoy the past because they have much more of it than they do of the future. But why analyze it? In my own case, and no doubt in that of many other collectors/readers, it is too interesting not to enjoy again and again. (Would one look at the Mona Lisa only once?) There is always the comfort of the known and the trusted.

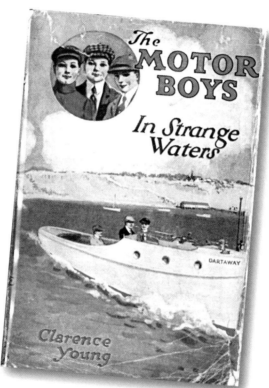

Motor Boys #7 from the Stratemeyer Syndicate in 1909.

One has to wonder who decided what the ages of potential readers were for the various series books. On Grosset & Dunlap book dust jackets, a number was given at the bottom for determining the age of the child the book was intended for. The number "80 – 110" on the Five Little Peppers series meant that the books were for children age eight to eleven. The Hardy Boys® books had the number "100 – 140," meaning ages ten to fourteen. This had to have been based on the subject matter, not the reading level. When I was twelve, I had some problems understanding situations and conversations in the Pepper books; I did not in the Hardy Boys® books. Even today I think that the language and style of the Five Little Peppers books is far in advance of an eight-year-old reader. The main determining factor of how many boys' or girls' series, also about people in their late teens or

older, is meant for youngsters is that there is never any mention of sexual conduct, overt violence or graphic situations.

Earlier in this chapter it was pointed out that which gives an old book its value. Another element that continues to interest and puzzle collectors of series books is the problem of "First Editions."

Such common statements as "probable first edition" constantly amuse all of us who collect the books and look for them on sales lists and on eBay. This is not an inaccurate statement. It is just terribly redundant. Case in point: The first Chip Hilton book, *Touchdown Pass*, is always a first edition. There was never any other edition, not counting the rewritten paperback book available now. Every single volume is the same edition. What the seller means is no doubt "First Printing." Who knows? This book was printed from 1948 through at least 1966, many different times. The problem is that many (if not most) of the people who have the book for sale do not understand much about books. If they see a copyright of 1948 on a book they assume that this very copy was printed in 1948, although there are two distinct formats for *The Touchdown Pass* and within each format there are a few variations. It is even possible that Grosset & Dunlap printed the book about twenty different times. Thus, series books are also distinct from many other books in that they were printed over and over for years and years. It is a real shame that the publishers did not list the number and the year of the printings on series books as was done on Little Golden Books. (On the other hand, it is bad enough that there are different formats to collect.)

Those who know anything about series books realize that the early format editions and later volumes in any given series are the most difficult ones to find today. The first 1927 printing of the initial Hardy Boys® book, *The Tower Treasure,* is very difficult to locate now. The last volume in a series, such as the Number 23 Chip Hilton, *Hungry Hurler,* was only printed once.

A last thought on collecting the sets of series books, as opposed to getting them just to read them: Would we bother to collect them if they were still available in retail outlets in their original presentation just like they were when we were young? Probably.

Common Abbreviations and Terms

Digest A paperback book that is about the same size as most series books (about 5 inches by 7 inches).

DJ; djs The protective paper dust jacket on a book.

Wrap DJ The picture on the front of the dust jacket wraps around the spine of the book and is part of it.

EP; eps Endpapers on a book. One side is glued to the hard cover; the other is the first "page" of the book. The eps are usually decorated.

Frontis The frontispiece is the first, and often only, illustration in a book.

Glossy frontis A frontispiece printed on thick, glossy paper. These were hand-tipped into books up until World War II.

Plain frontis The frontispiece is printed on the same paper as the rest of the book and is usually a line drawing, like the pictures in coloring books.

Internals The illustrations inside a series book, usually placed at equal intervals throughout the text. They were usually glossy and had to be hand-tipped in, like the glossy frontis, and were used mostly before World War II.

Mass-market This refers to the common size paperback book, which is usually about 4 inches by 6 inches

PB A paperback book.

PC A picture cover book. The picture is printed as part of the covering over the composition or cardboard that makes up the hard covers of the book. Some PCs are made as part of the book; others have a layer of cellophane (which can become loose) over the picture.

Formats

The "Formats" used for each series of books is a way to designate the differences among them. Books and pamphlets have already established Formats for some of these boys' series books, but I have used my own system, which is less complicated than some others already in print. I find it easier to do it this way instead of breaking each series down into such specific components that it is difficult to determine some of the minor differences between them. The "Formatting" used here divides each series into differences which are obvious and each is explained for the series that it represents. This formatting system is not meant to contradict others in use; it is meant as an aid in establishing prices for the books and as a way to build uniform collections of a certain series, although that is not always possible either. The serious collector is encouraged to purchase the more detailed books about a series such as the Hardy Boys®.

AtlanticRichfield [sic] advertisement for the Hardy Boys® and Nancy Drew® book club in the late 1970s.

Chapter 2

Edward Stratemeyer

Edward Stratemeyer.

Edward Stratemeyer (1862-1930) grew up in the era when Americans were taught that there was no accomplishment to which they could not aspire. The period in American history after the Civil War, especially in the victorious North, was one in which life was changing rapidly as Americans by the thousands left the countryside to move to the cities where opportunities were limitless. It was the age of Carnegie, Rockefeller, Morgan and many others who made it big in a big way. It was the era in which Horatio Alger wrote dozens of books proving how "living right paid off." At least it seemed this way, and Stratemeyer must have believed it was. He did not become successful with iron and steel, oil or finance; he did become the most prolific American writer and/or book producer of all time. Yet he was never blamed for creating a monopoly, as were the "robber barons" of the era.

Stratemeyer, who had only an eighth-grade education, was a voracious reader of the juvenile literature of his time. Imitating the popular works he preferred, he wrote and published his first story in the boys' magazine *Golden Days* in 1889, for which he received $75, a goodly amount of money then. He was later hired by Street and Smith, publishers of dime novels and fiction magazines, where he met his childhood idols, Oliver Optic and Horatio Alger, Jr., the authors of the "living right pays off" juvenile novels he read as a youth. At Street and Smith, Stratemeyer edited and finished the books Alger and Optic had not completed at the time of their deaths and he also wrote at least eleven new volumes under the Alger name.

From 1894 to 1908, Stratemeyer wrote about seventy-five boys' books in several different series and these were published under his own name by various companies that concentrated on the juvenile market, such as Lothrop, Lee & Shephard. These books were about boys and their adventures, success stories of the Alger type and patriotic volumes dealing with American bravery in the Revolution and other wars. The most successful of these books was *Under Dewey at Manila*, published in 1898 at the time of the American victory over Spain in a brief and popular war.

Around 1906, Stratemeyer formed a syndicate to complete all the book ideas he was developing. It is estimated that he personally wrote about 200 books and that he outlined and edited another few hundred that were finished by ghostwriters. The most popular of these were Tom Swift®, the Rover Boys, the Bobbsey Twins, Baseball Joe, the Outdoor Girls, Ruth Fielding, Honey Bunch, Bomba the Jungle Boy, Nancy Drew® and the Hardy Boys®. Stratemeyer created many pen names for the "authors" of these series books. Many of the names had obvious meanings, such as Arthur M. Winfield, the "author" of the Rover Boys books. Arthur is a homonym for author, "M" is for the millions (of books or dollars) hoped for and "Winfield" stood for success.

No one person could produce all the books Stratemeyer had in mind so he hired writers who finished books that he plotted and outlined and they were published under "house names." A good example of this is Laura Lee Hope, author of the Bobbsey Twins books, the longest running Stratemeyer series, which was published from 1904 until about 1990. Many different writers worked on this list and on "Miss Hope's" other works, such as the Six Little Bunkers, the Outdoor Girls and the Moving Picture Girls. Ghostwriters who filled in the details of the stories were paid a flat rate of about $75 to $100 (some writers probably commanded more) for each completed 200-page book. Lately there has been a great number of articles and books decrying the practice of paying the ghostwriters so little. How long would it require to write a Bobbsey Twins book in 1925? Two weeks? A month? At any rate, the number of words in the book was less than the average newspaper reporter wrote in a week for a salary of about $20 per week. A certain amount of talent and imagination was required to fill in the details of a Stratemeyer Syndicate book, but the real credit does seem to belong to Edward Stratemeyer and his successors who provided most of the creativity.

Some of the most important Stratemeyer writers were the ones who worked on the three most enduring series. These are Howard R. Garis who wrote about twenty-five Bobbsey Twins books and thirty-five Tom Swift® ones; Mildred A. Wirt who created several of the Ruth Fielding,

Nancy Drew®, and Kay Tracey books; and Leslie McFarlane who did the Hardy Boys® books for the first twenty years. The identities of these authors were kept secret (by contract) for most of the 20th century.

Another Stratemeyer invention was the 50-cent book. In 1906, a Five Little Peppers book from Lothrop, Lee & Shephard cost $1.50; other publishers' juvenile series were priced about the same. Cupples & Leon's and Grosset & Dunlap's 50-cent Stratemeyer books had heavy cloth-covered covers, a full color dust jacket, from one to four internal illustrations, heavy acid-free paper, and clear typesetting with large print. Librarians considered none of these books "literature" and they were not found in public libraries until very recently. This factor probably caused more books to be sold than anything else, as young people loved them and wanted to read them. The volume of old copies still available for collectors proves that many millions were printed. All of the Stratemeyer Syndicate books showed several generations of juveniles a positive, affirmative, and enthusiastic view of American life. They always gave hope for a promising future and, like Alger's books, proved that "living right pays." It is true that there were racial and ethnic stereotypes in the books, but there were probably less than in adult fiction of the same period.

The Stratemeyer Syndicate supplied the publishing houses that catered to the juvenile market, such as Cupples & Leon and Grosset & Dunlap, with product during the entire 20th century. Mr. Stratemeyer was always astute in designing new series books and addressed the popular adult trends by creating a similar juvenile market. Examples of this are Bomba the Jungle Boy, an obvious Tarzan-type; all the Moving Picture series of the period in which the movies were developing as popular entertainment; and the teenage detectives like Nancy Drew® and the Hardy Boys® who were introduced at the time of rising popularity in adult detective fiction.

When Stratemeyer died in 1930, his daughters, Harriet Stratemeyer Adams and Edna Stratemeyer Squier, continued with his work and the Stratemeyer Syndicate, consolidating the policies begun by their father.

Early Series Books by Edward Stratemeyer

Series	Dates	Volumes
Bound to Succeed	1894-1899	3
Ship and Shore	1894-1900	3
Bound to Win	1897	12
Working Upwards	1897	4
Minute Boys	1898-1912	11
Old Glory	1898-1901	6
Soldiers of Fortune	1900-1906	4
American Boys Biographical	1901-1904	2
Colonial (French & Indian War)	1901-1906	6
Pan-American	1902-1911	6
Great American Industries	1903	1
Dave Porter	1905-1919	15
Lakeport	1908-1912	6

Stratemeyer Series by Pseudonyms and Ghostwriters

Series	Author	Dates	Volumes
Young Sportsmen	Capt. Ralph Bonehill	1897	3
Flag of Freedom	Capt. Ralph Bonehill	1899-1902	6
Rover Boys	Arthur M. Winfield	1899-1926	30
Young Hunters	Capt. Ralph Bonehill	1900	2
Mexican War Series	Capt. Ralph Bonehill	1900-1902	3
Putnam Hall	Arthur M. Winfield	1901-1911; 1921	6
Frontier Series	Capt. Ralph Bonehill	1903-1906	3

Series	Author	Dates	Volumes
Bobbsey Twins®	Laura Lee Hope	1904+	72+
Deep Sea	Roy Rockwood	1905-1908	4
Dave Fearless	Roy Rockwood	1905-1927	17
Boy Hunters	Capt. Ralph Bonehill	1906-1910	4
Boys of Business	Allen Chapman	1906-1911	5
Motor Boys	Clarence Young	1906-1924	22
Ralph (Railroad)	Allen Chapman	1906-1928	10
Great Marvel	Roy Rockwood	1906-1935	9
Jack Ranger	Clarence Young	1907-1911	6
Darewell Chums	Allen Chapman	1908-1911	5
Dorothy Dale	Margaret Penrose	1908-1924	13
The Webster Series	Frank V. Webster	1909-1915; 1938	25
College Sports	Lester Chadwick	1910-1913	6
Motor Girls	Margaret Penrose	1910-1917	10
Tom Swift®	Victor Appleton	1910-1941	40
Boys of Columbia High	Graham B. Forbes	1911-1920	8
Racer Boys	Clarence Young	1912-1914	6
Fairview Boys	Frederick Gordon	1912-1917	6
Baseball Joe	Lester Chadwick	1912-1928	14
Fred Fenton	Allen Chapman	1913-1915	5
Dave Dashaway	Roy Rockwood	1913-1915	5
Tom Fairfield	Allen Chapman	1913-1915	5
Motion Picture Chums	Victor Appleton	1913-1916	7
Moving Picture Boys	Victor Appleton	1913-1922	10
Outdoor Girls	Laura Lee Hope	1913-1933	23
Ruth Fielding	Alice B. Emerson	1913-1934	30
Speedwell Boys	Roy Rockwood	1913-1915	5
Moving Picture Girls	Laura Lee Hope	1914-1916	7
Corner House Girls	Grace Brooks Hill	1915-1926	13
White Ribbon Boys	Raymond Sperry, Jr.	1916	1
YMCA Boys	Brooks Henerley	1916-1917	3
Bunny Brown and His Sister Sue	Laura Lee Hope	1916-1931	?
Nan Sherwood	Annie Roe Carr	1916-1937	7
Six Little Bunkers	Laura Lee Hope	1918-1930	?
Betty Gordon	Alice B. Emerson	1920-1932	15
Billie Bradley	Janet D. Wheeler	1920-1932	9
Make-Believe Stories	Laura Lee Hope	1920-1923	12+(?)
Four Little Blossoms	Mabel C. Hawley	1920-1930; 1938	?
Radio Boys	Allen Chapman	1922-1930	13
Radio Girls	Margaret Penrose	1922-1924	4
Honey Bunch	Helen Louise Thorndyke	1923-1955	32
Blythe Girls	Laura Lee Hope	1925-1932	12
Don Sturdy	Victor Appleton	1925-1935	15
Flyaways	Alice Dale Hardy	1925	?
The X Bar X Boys	James Cody Ferris	1926-1942	22
Bomba the Jungle Boy	Roy Rockwood	1926-1938; 1953	20

Series	Author	Dates	Volumes
Frank Allen	Graham B. Forbes	1926-1927	17
Garry Grayson (Football)	Elmer Dawson	1926-1932	10
Hardy Boys®	Franklin W. Dixon	1927+	100+
Ted Scott	Franklin W. Dixon	1927-1943	20
Roy Stover	Philip A. Bartlett	1929-1934	4
Nancy Drew®	Carolyn Keene	1930+	100+
Buck and Larry (Baseball)	Elmer Dawson	1930-1932	5
Doris Force	Julia K. Duncan	1931-1932	4
Jerry Ford	Fenworth Moore	1931-1932; 1937	4
Perry Pierce	Clinton W. Locke	1931-1934	4
Dana Girls	Carolyn Keene	1934-1979	34
Kay Tracey	Frances K Judd	1934-1942; 1951-1953; 1978; 1980	18
Happy Hollisters	Jerry West	1953-1970; 1979	33
Tom Swift, Jr.	Victor Appleton II	1954-1971	33
Honey Bunch and Norman	Helen Louise Thorndyke	1957-1963	12
Bret King	Dan Scott	1960-1964	9
Linda Craig	Ann Sheldon	1962-1964; 1981	11
		1988-1990	12
Christopher Cool	Jack Lancer	1967-1969	6
Tolliver Adventure Series	Alan Stone	1967	3
Tom Swift® (III)	Victor Appleton	1981-1984	11
Tom Swift® (IV)	Victor Appleton	1991-1993	13
Hardy Boys® & Tom Swift®	Franklin W. Dixon	1992-1993	2

Dave Porter

The Dave Porter Series has the distinction of being the one with the most volumes carrying Edward Stratemeyer's name. There were fifteen books between 1905 and 1919. Dave's adventures center around life and sports at Oak Hall boarding school, his travels to exotic locations, and his many interesting adventures. Stratemeyer tells in the preface to *Dave Porter in the Far North* that his hero is "bright, manly, and honest to the core, and in those qualities I trust my young readers will take him as their model throughout life."

The Dave Porter books were published by Lothrop, Lee & Shephard in thick editions of about 300 pages each with eight glossy illustrations by important illustrators such as Walter S. Rogers.

Dave Porter Book Formats, 1905-1919

I. #1 – #15
Cloth binding, each with a different color picture.
Front and spine have shield reading "Dave Porter Series."
Glossy frontis and seven glossy internals
DJ matches cover

II. #1 – #15
Green cloth binding with picture of Dave in center, surrounded by four small figures; spine has scroll reading "Dave Porter Series – Special Edition;" red ink used in the pictures
Glossy frontis and seven glossy internals
DJ shows Dave carrying a valise

III. #1 – #15	IV. #1 – #15
Orange-yellow cloth binding with same design as Format II, except only black ink used Glossy frontis and seven glossy internals DJ shows head of Dave in an oval with scenes surrounding him	Same as Format III, except binding may also be tan and four internals have been omitted.

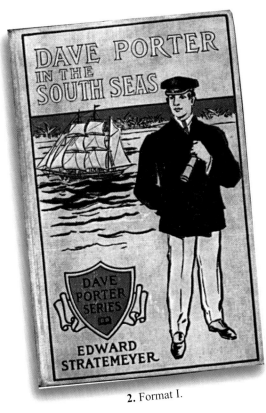

2. Format I.

11. Format II DJ.

11. Format III.

Values for Dave Porter Books

All Formats $10.00-$45.00

Year	Volume
1905	**1. Dave Porter at Oak Hall or, the School Days of an American Boy**
1906	**2. Dave Porter in the South Seas or, The Strange Cruise of the Stormy Petrel**
1907	**3. Dave Porter's Return to School or, Winning the Medal of Honor**
1908	**4. Dave Porter in the Far North or, The Pluck of an American Schoolboy**
1909	**5. Dave Porter and His Classmates or, For the Honor of Oak Hall**
1910	**6. Dave Porter at Star Ranch or, The Cowboy's Secret**
1911	**7. Dave Porter and His Rivals or, The Chums and Foes of Oak Hall**
1912	**8. Dave Porter on Cave Island or, A Schoolboy's Mysterious Mission**
1913	**9. Dave Porter and the Runaways or, Last Days at Oak Hall**
1914	**10. Dave Porter in the Gold Fields or, The Search for the Landslide Mine**
1915	**11. Dave Porter at Bear Camp or, The Wild Man of Mirror Lake**
1916	**12. Dave Porter and His Double or, The Disappearance of the Basswood Fortune**
1917	**13. Dave Porter's Great Search or, The Perils of a Young Civil Engineer**
1918	**14. Dave Porter Under Fire or, A Young Army Engineer in France**
1919	**15. Dave Porter's War Honors or, At the Front with the Fighting Engineers**

The Rover Boys

The first Stratemeyer series that was successful for many years is the Rover Boys, written under the name Arthur M. Winfield from 1899 to 1926. There are thirty volumes in the series. The first twenty books are about the adventures of Dick, Tom and Sam Rover; the last ten are called the Second Rover Boys Series and are about their four sons, Jack, Fred and the twins Randy and Andy. The early volumes about the Rovers detail the adventures of their travels. Most of the later books concentrate on mystery and suspense. Like the Dave Porter series, the author has an introduction to explain that the book is complete in itself but it is also part of a larger series of similar books. "Winfield" also mentioned how much he treasured all the letters he received about his books. These volumes were written in the era when the author would also address the "kind reader" of them in the narrative portion of the book. From 1901 to 1911 Winfield also wrote the Putnam Hall Series of six books to tell what happened at the boarding school previous to the arrival of the Rover brothers.

The Rover Boys series had many different publishers. Among them were the Mershon Co., Stitt Publishing Co., Chatterton-Peck Co., Grosset & Dunlap, and Whitman. The Rover Boys books are about 150 pages long.

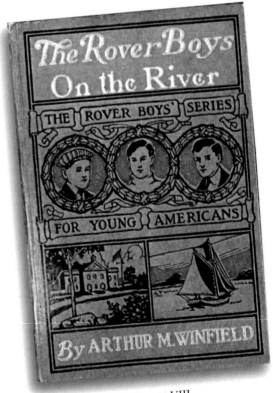

9. Format VIII.

The Rover Boys Book Formats

I. 1899 – 1904 The Mershon Co.
#1 – #8
Light green cloth with red lettering
Picture of three boys' heads in circles in a row with white background
Glossy frontis and three glossy internals
DJ matches cover

II. 1905 The Stitt Co.
#1 – #9, including first printing of #9
Same as Format I, except "Stitt" is on spine

III. 1905 – 1906 The Mershon Co.
#1 – #11, including first printing of #10 and #11
Same as Format I, with Mershon Co. on spine

IV. 1906 – 1907 Chatterton-Peck Co.
#1 – #11
Same as Format I with "C.P. Co." on spine

V. 1906 – 1907 Chatterton-Peck Co.
#1 – #11
Red or green cloth library binding with picture of full-length view of the boys
Illustrations and djs same as Format I

VI. 1907 Grosset & Dunlap
#1 – #11
Same as Format I with "Grosset & Dunlap" on spine

VII. 1908 Grosset & Dunlap
#1 – #13, including first printing of #12 and #13
Similar to Format I with "Grosset & Dunlap" on spine

VIII. 1909 – 1916 Grosset & Dunlap
#1 – #20, including first printings of #14 – #20
Dark green cloth book with white titles; the three portraits in circles are updated and have red backgrounds
Glossy frontis and three glossy internals
DJ matches cover

IX. 1917 – 1919 Grosset & Dunlap
#21 – #22, first printings of Second Rover Boys Series
Like Format VIII with red lettering; four ovals with heads of the four Rover sons
Glossy frontis and three glossy internals
DJ matches cover

X. 1919 – 1931 Grosset & Dunlap
#1 – #30, including first printings of #23 – #30
Tan cloth cover with red letters; red and brown pictures of the four boys
Glossy frontis and three glossy internals
DJ of Format VIII; in mid-1920s dj became full color, showing three boys and two small scenes

XI. 1932+ Grosset & Dunlap
#1 – #30
Orange or red cloth cover; plain with design on front
Glossy frontis and three glossy internals
DJ is 1920s design in full color

XII. 1940s Whitman Publishing Co.
Eight volumes – The original #1; #2; #7; #8; #10; #11; #13; and #14
Composition bindings in various colors
No illustrations
New dj in color; different for each volume

Values for The Rover Boys Books

Formats I. to XI.	$3.00-$45.00+
Format XII.	$3.00-$18.00

Year	Volume
1899	**1. The Rover Boys at School or, The Cadets of Putnam Hall**
1899	**2. The Rover Boys on the Ocean or, A Chase for a Fortune**
1899	**3. The Rover Boys in the Jungle or, Stirring Adventures in Africa**
1900	**4. The Rover Boys Out West or, The Search for a Lost Mine**
1901	**5. The Rover Boys on the Great Lakes or, The Secret of the Island Cave**
1902	**6. The Rover Boys in the Mountains or, A Hunt for Fame and Fortune**
1903	**7. The Rover Boys on Land and Sea or, The Crusoes of Seven Islands**
1904	**8. The Rover Boys in Camp or, The Rivals of Pine Island**
1905	**9. The Rover Boys on the River or, The Search for the Missing Houseboat**
1906	**10. The Rover Boys on the Plains or, The Mystery of Red Rock Ranch**

Year	Volume
1907	11. The Rover Boys in Southern Waters or, The Deserted Steam Yacht
1908	12. The Rover Boys on the Farm or, The Last Days at Putnam Hall
1909	13. The Rover Boys on Treasure Isle or, The Strange Cruise of the Steam Yacht
1910	14. The Rover Boys at College or, The Right Road and the Wrong
1911	15. The Rover Boys Down East or, The Struggle for the Stanhope Fortune
1912	16. The Rover Boys in the Air or, From College Campus to the Clouds
1913	17. The Rover Boys in New York or, Saving Their Father's Honor
1914	18. The Rover Boys in Alaska or, Lost in the Fields of Ice
1915	19. The Rover Boys in Business or, The Search for the Missing Bonds
1916	20. The Rover Boys on a Tour or, Last Days at Brill College
1917	21. The Rover Boys at Colby Hall or, The Struggle of the Young Cadets
1918	22. The Rover Boys on Snowshoe Island or, The Old Lumberman's Treasure Box
1919	23. The Rover Boys Under Canvas or, The Mystery of the Wrecked Submarine
1920	24. The Rover Boys on a Hunt or, The Mysterious House in the Woods
1921	25. The Rover Boys in the Land of Luck or, Stirring Adventures in the Oil Fields
1922	26. The Rover Boys at Big Horn Ranch or, The Cowboys' Double Roundup
1923	27. The Rover Boys at Big Bear Lake or, The Camps of the Rival Cadets
1924	28. The Rover Boys Shipwrecked or, A Thrilling Hunt for Pirates' Gold
1925	29. The Rover Boys on Sunset Trail or, The Old Miner's Mysterious Message
1926	30. The Rover Boys Winning a Fortune or, Strenuous Days Afloat and Ashore

Putnam Hall Book Formats

From 1901 to 1906 Volumes 1 and 2 were published by the Mershon Co., Stitt Publishing Co., and Chatterton-Peck Co. Each of these three formats was a gray cloth book with a picture of cadets on parade on the cover and an orange sword on the spine. Grosset & Dunlap took over the series and had three distinct formats. The fourth format is the same as the above. The fifth had the artwork in black only. The final format was the same as the second Grosset & Dunlap version, except the titles were reversed. For example, in the sixth format *The Putnam Hall Rivals* became *The Rivals of Putnam Hall*.

Values for Putnam Hall Books

All formats $3.00-$50.00+

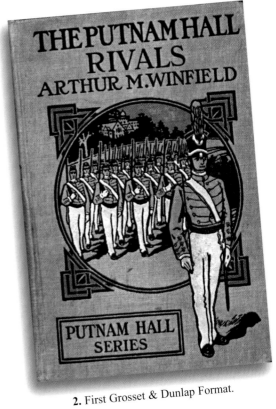

2. First Grosset & Dunlap Format.

Year	Volume
1901	1. The Putnam Hall Cadets or, Good Times In School and Out
1906	2. The Putnam Hall Rivals or, Fun and Sport Afloat and Ashore
1908	3. The Putnam Hall Champions or, Bound to Win Out
1909	4. The Putnam Hall Rebellion or, The Rival Runaways
1910	5. The Putnam Hall Encampment or, The Secret of the Old Mill
1911	6. The Putnam Hall Mystery or, The School Chums Strange Discovery

Chapter 3

Tom Swift® and Other Scientists

Grosset & Dunlap

By the early 1900s the most important Stratemeyer books were published by Grosset & Dunlap, although other publishing houses also printed many of the Syndicate's books. The successors to the original Grosset & Dunlap company still print the classic, or original, Hardy Boys® and Nancy Drew® books.

Grosset & Dunlap is the favorite publisher of everyone who collects series books. The company's products from the beginning of the 20th century until the early 1990s are the books that are the most collected and respected now. This is because of the nice presentation of the books, with their cheerful and colorful dust jackets and covers and the fact that the most popular and well-remembered series characters came from this company.

Grosset & Dunlap was founded in 1898 when partners George Dunlap and Alex Grosset went into business in New York. At first the company published reprints for the adult market. The first successful juvenile series was Edward Stratemeyer's Tom Swift®, which began in 1910. By 1950 Grosset & Dunlap was the leading publisher of juvenile books in the United States, but it began to decline in importance after that point and later became a part of Filmways, an entertainment company, and then G.P. Putnam's Sons Publishers.

In 1979 the Stratemeyer Syndicate switched from Grosset & Dunlap, with whom it had been associated for about seventy years, to Simon & Schuster. This meant that Grosset & Dunlap lost its important series books – The Hardy Boys®, Nancy Drew® and the Bobbsey Twins. In 1982, a court decision gave Grosset & Dunlap the rights to the Stratemeyer books that it had published up to 1979 and Simon & Schuster took over the three successful series and produced them as paperbacks with many titles in each set released per year. In 1984 Simon & Schuster purchased the Stratemeyer Syndicate.

As of this writing, there are still Grosset & Dunlap hardback picture cover books of the first fifty-eight Hardy Boys® and the first fifty-six Nancy Drew® titles. The Bobbsey Twins books were discontinued in about 1998 after having been in production for almost one hundred years. It is probably just a matter of time before the Hardy Boys® and Nancy Drew® will end as Grosset & Dunlap series also, as the same volumes with very little change in design have been marketed from 1987 until the present time. I have noticed that many of the chain bookstores that always stocked great quantities of the Grosset & Dunlap books no longer carry a wide selection of them.

Tom Swift®, 1910-1935

Tom Swift® is one of Edward Stratemeyer's most famous inventions. The series lasted essentially from 1910 until the mid-1990s, rivaling the Bobbsey Twins for longevity. There are five distinct sets of Tom Swift® books.

Tom Swift® of the first series (1910 to 1941) was a teenage boy who had a tremendous knowledge of scientific development and invention based on personal observation and experimentation. He lived in upstate New York. (The Bobbsey Twins books seemed to be set here also.) Dave Porter and the Rover Boys did get as far away from home as the South Seas and Africa but Tom went under the land, under the seas, and into the skies. Tom Swift® had many interesting adventures. He had his share of problems also, but with invention and wit escaped from peril and disaster, whether it was a quick save with his motorcycle, his adeptness at handling a motorboat, or his expertise with flying machines.

Stratemeyer's book-writing syndicate was firmly in place by the time he developed the series about a boy inventor. It is believed that the actual writer of the original thirty-eight volumes in the series was Howard R. Garis. Victor Appleton, the Stratemeyer name for the author of the books, used more and more "Tom Swifties" as the series progressed. These are sentence constructions in which new adverbs were formed from verbs, such as "Tom said soothingly" and other clever wording such as "Tom Swift® quickly hurried to the engine room." (*Undersea Search*, page 115.) Garis had fun creating these witticisms, as well as the hair-raising situations in which Tom found himself.

Howard R. Garis

Howard R. Garis was about as prolific a writer of series books as Edward Stratemeyer. Garis was born in Binghamton, New York, in 1873; he died in 1962. He began his writing career as a reporter for newspapers. By 1908 he was working for the Stratemeyer Syndicate. Not only did he write the Tom Swift® books, but under other Stratemeyer "house names" he also did many volumes of the Motor Boys, Baseball Joe, The Outdoor Girls, The Bobbsey Twins, Bunny Brown and His Sister Sue, and other series. Under his own name he wrote the Buddy series, the Curlytops series, and his most famous one – Uncle Wiggily, countless tales of a sprightly rabbit.

In the biography of Howard Garis, *My Father Was Uncle Wiggily* (McGraw-Hill, 1966), Roger Garis told how his father had prodigious energy and that he never got tired. He also wrote at great speed and would complete a series book for Stratemeyer in six to eight days. In 1900 Howard Garis married Lilian McNamara (born 1872) who wrote series books and other girls' books under the name Lilian Garis. Garis' son Roger and daughter Cleo also wrote for the Stratemeyer Syndicate. The four Garis writers produced more than one thousand books for children. Howard Garis also designed the Uncle Wiggily board game and other Uncle Wiggily toys and merchandise.

Roger Garis' book about his father was the first time that much information was available about the Stratemeyer Syndicate and its writers and the methods used to produce the many series books that it had published. At this time, most people still believed that a real Victor Appleton had written the Tom Swift® books and that Franklin W. Dixon was the actual author of the Hardy Boys® series. In 1976 Canadian writer Leslie McFarlane published *Ghost of the Hardy Boys®* about his authorship of the early books in this series, breaking another vow of silence about the Syndicate. It was not until after the death of Harriet Stratemeyer Adams in 1982 that the Syndicate itself was willing to reveal the names of the actual authors of its books. The publicity from the 1982 court decision concerning Grosset & Dunlap and the Syndicate because of the switch to Simon & Schuster as publisher in 1979 ended the mystique that Edward Stratemeyer had developed around his company.

Illustrators

H. Rudolph Mencl illustrated the first five books. Volumes 6 through 16 were by H. Richard Boehm. Volumes 17 through 20 and 24 through 34 were by Walter S. Rogers. In between, R. Emmett Owen did volumes 21, 22 and 23. Volumes 35 through 38 have illustrations by Nat Falk.

Tom Swift® Book Formats

Grosset & Dunlap

I. 1910 – 1917
#1 – #20, including first printings #1 – #20
Finely woven tan cloth binding; front and spine in black and red; front has oval with title and four pictures at each corner, called "The Four Square" or "Quad" design
Plain eps; glossy frontis
#1 – #5 have unvarnished tan dj with red lettering and artwork
#6 – #10 and reprints have unvarnished tan dj with red lettering and red and green artwork
#11 – #20 and reprints have varnished dj with red lettering and red and green artwork

II. 1918 – 1933, including first printings #21 – #35
#1 – #35
Coarsely woven light tan cloth binding with design as in Format I (#34 and #35 can be gray-tan)
Plain eps; glossy frontis
#21 – #26 and reprints have orange and gray picture on dj, a "duotone" version of frontis
#27 – #35 and reprints have full color dj; spine logo picture of Tom is modernized

III. 1933 – 1935, including first printings #36 – #38
 #1 – #38, including first editions of #36 – #38
 Plain orange cloth with black lettering
 Orange illustrated eps; glossy frontis
 #1 – #36 have full color djs with another new
   spine logo of Tom Swift®, showing him smiling
 #37 – #38 have cartoon-like dj pictures

See the listing following for the above thirty-eight
Tom Swift® books.

Whitman Publishing Co. "Better Little Book"

IV. 1939 – 1941
 These are thick little books, like the "Big Little
   Books" and measure 4½ inches by 3-5/8 inches
 Cardboard picture covers in color

1485. *Tom Swift® and His Giant Telescope* (1939)
1437. *Tom Swift® and His Magnetic Silencer* (1941)

Whitman Publishing Co. reprints

V. 1940s
 Last ten Grosset & Dunlap titles in a different
   order
 Cloth or composition cover, various colors
 Color dj; no illustrations

2160. *Tom Swift® and His Television Detector*
2161. *Tom Swift® and His House on Wheels*
2162. *Tom Swift® and His Sky Train*
2163. *Tom Swift® and Circling the Globe*
2164. *Tom Swift® and His Ocean Airport*
2165. *Tom Swift® and His Planet Stone*
2166. *Tom Swift® and His Airline Express*
2167. *Tom Swift® and His Talking Pictures*
2168. *Tom Swift® and His Big Dirigible*
2169. *Tom Swift® and His Giant Magnet*

Applewood Books

VI. 1992
 #1 – #3
 Reprints that are similar in presentation to Format
   II

Values for Tom Swift® Books

Format I.	$2.00-$50.00+
Format II.	$2.00-$50.00+
Format III.	$2.00-$70.00+
Volumes 23 – 32	$4.00-$200.00
Volumes 33 – 36	$10.00-$250.00
Volume 37	$10.00-$500.00+
Volume 38	$10.00-$1500.00+
Format IV.	$1.00-$45.00+
Format V.	$1.00-$35.00
Format VI.	retail

Year	Volume
1910	**1. Tom Swift® and His Motor Cycle or, Fun and Adventure on the Road**
1910	**2. Tom Swift® and His Motor Boat or, The Rivals of Lake Carlopa**
1910	**3. Tom Swift® and His Air Ship or, The Stirring Cruise of the Red Cloud**
1910	**4. Tom Swift® and His Submarine or, Under the Ocean for Sunken Treasure**
1910	**5. Tom Swift® and His Electric Runabout or, The Speediest Car on the Road**
1911	**6. Tom Swift® and His Wireless Message or, The Castaways of Earthquake Island**
1911	**7. Tom Swift® Among the Diamond Makers or, The Secret of Phantom Mountain**
1911	**8. Tom Swift® in the Caves of Ice or, The Wreck of the Airship**
1911	**9. Tom Swift® and His Sky Racer or, The Quickest Flight on Record**
1911	**10. Tom Swift® and His Electric Rifle or, Daring Adventures in Elephant Land**
1912	**11. Tom Swift® in the City of Gold or, Marvelous Adventures Underground**
1912	**12. Tom Swift® and His Air Glider or, Seeking the Platinum Treasure**
1912	**13. Tom Swift® in Captivity or, A Daring Escape by Airship**
1912	**14. Tom Swift® and His Wizard Camera or, Thrilling Adventures While Taking Moving Pictures**

1. Full color DJ.

6. Full color DJ.

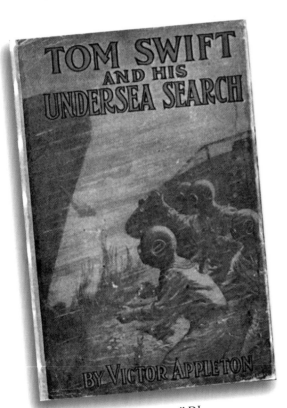

23. "Duotone" DJ.

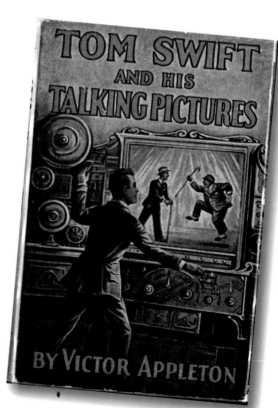

31. Full color DJ.

Year	Volume
1912	15. Tom Swift® and His Great Searchlight or, On the Border for Uncle Sam
1913	16. Tom Swift® and His Giant Cannon or, The Longest Shots on Record
1914	17. Tom Swift® and His Photo Telephone or, The Picture That Saved a Fortune
1915	18. Tom Swift® and His Aerial Warship or, The Naval Terror of the Seas
1916	19. Tom Swift® and His Big Tunnel or, The Hidden City of the Andes
1917	20. Tom Swift® in the Land of Wonders or, The Search for the Idol of Gold
1918	21. Tom Swift® and His War Tank or, Doing His Bit for Uncle Sam
1919	22. Tom Swift® and His Air Scout or, Uncle Sam's Mastery of the Sky
1920	23. Tom Swift® and His Undersea Search or, The Treasure on the Floor of the Atlantic
1921	24. Tom Swift® Among the Fire Fighters or, Battling with Flames From the Air
1922	25. Tom Swift® and His Electric Locomotive or, Two Miles a Minute on the Rails
1923	26. Tom Swift® and His Flying Boat or, The Castaways of the Giant Iceberg
1924	27. Tom Swift® and His Great Oil Gusher or, The Treasure of Goby Farm
1925	28. Tom Swift® and His Chest of Secrets or, Tracing the Stolen Inventions
1926	29. Tom Swift® and His Airline Express or, From Ocean to Ocean by Daylight
1927	30. Tom Swift® Circling the Globe or, The Daring Cruise of the Air Monarch
1928	31. Tom Swift® and His Talking Pictures or, The Greatest Invention on Record
1929	32. Tom Swift® and His House on Wheels or, A Trip to the Mountain of Mystery
1930	33. Tom Swift® and His Big Dirigible or, Adventures Over the Forest of Fire
1931	34. Tom Swift® and His Sky Train or, Overland Through the Clouds
1932	35. Tom Swift® and His Giant Magnet or, Bringing Up the Lost Submarine
1933	36. Tom Swift® and His Television Detector or, Trailing the Secret Plotters
1934	37. Tom Swift® and His Ocean Airport or, Foiling the Haargolanders
1935	38. Tom Swift® and His Planet Stone or, Discovering the Secret of Another World

Tom Swift Jr.

From 1954 to 1978 Grosset & Dunlap published another Stratemeyer series of Tom Swift® books. This set was called The New Tom Swift Jr. Adventures and was "by Victor Appleton II." In the stories, Tom Jr. is the son of the original Tom Swift®; the author is presumably the son of the original Victor Appleton, as this was still in the era when the identities of Stratemeyer ghostwriters were well kept secrets. The original outlines for the Tom Swift Jr. books are supposed to have been created by Edward Stratemeyer's daughter Harriet and Syndicate writers filled in the details. In the second Tom Swift® series the plots concentrate on Tom's fantastic inventions and his explorations all over the earth and into outer space. The titles of the books in the series show what sort of inventions Tom came up with. His best friend Bud Barclay, who dated Tom's sister Sandy, accompanied Tom on his adventures. Another character who went along on these expeditions is the comical Texan Chow Winkler, the cook.

The American Space Program of the 1950s and 1960s no doubt inspired the adventures that Tom Swift Jr. had. Tom got to the moon in 1958; real astronauts had to wait another eleven years. It is amazing that the Tom Swift Jr. series ended shortly after the American Moon Landing, as there should have been great interest at the time in a high quality boys' series about space exploration, like the new Tom Swift® one.

James Duncan Lawrence was the author of most of the Tom Swift Jr. books. He wrote twenty-four of the thirty-three titles. Graham Kaye painted the pictures for the first seventeen books that came with dust jackets and several other artists did them for the picture cover books that followed. The logo picture of Tom Jr. on the spine of the books is Kaye's work.

After the Tom Swift Jr. series of hardback books ended in 1971, Grosset & Dunlap attempted to continue it with the publication of a set of paperback books in 1972 and another paperback set in 1977. Grosset & Dunlap published the paperback books under a company division called Tempo, which also printed other series books, such as Judy Bolton, Cherry Ames, and Connie Blair, to prolong them in an economical way. These Tempo books attempted to play down the "Jr." element of Tom Swift's® name. All the paperback Tom Swift Jr. books are printed with the same plates as the original hardback books.

There were also foreign editions of the Tom Swift Jr. series. Among them were volumes from France, Denmark, and Iceland, translated into these respective languages.

Ghostwriter

1	William Dougherty
2 – 3	John Almquist
4	Richard Sklar
5 – 7	James Lawrence
8	Thomas Mulvey
9 – 29	James Lawrence
30	Thomas Mulvey
31 – 32	Richard McKenna
33	Vincent Buranelli

Illustrator

1 – 17	Graham Kaye
18 – 24	Charles Brey
25 – 26	Edward Moritz
27	Charles Brey
28 – 32	Ray Johnson
33	Bill Dolwick

Tom Swift Jr. Book Formats

Grosset & Dunlap

I. 1954 – 1961, including first printings #1 – #17
    #1 – #17
    Blue tweed composition binding
    Blue and white eps showing Tom in his lab
    Frontis and eight to eleven black and white line
       drawings
    Full color dj (see **Ghostwriter/Illustrator** for
       illustrators)

II. 1961
    #1 – #18, including first printing #18
    Blue spine picture cover; composition binding
    #18 has wrap spine picture, like wrap spine djs
    Illustrations same as Format I

III. 1962 – 1971, including first printing #19 – #33
    #1 – #33
    Yellow-orange spine picture cover; composition
       binding, as Format II

EPS of last printings are black and white version
   of scene of Tom in his lab
Illustrations same as Format I

Tempo (Grosset & Dunlap)

IV. 1972
    #1 – #4
    Digest-size paperback
    Books #14 – #17 are renumbered #1 – #4 with
       new titles for #14 and #15
    New cover art; frontis and internals from the
       originals

V. 1977
    #1 – #6
    Mass-market paperback
    Books #1 – #4, #6 and #8 are renumbered,
       #1 – #6, with #5 (former #6) retitled
    Third cover art; new inside illustrations by Tony
       Tallarico

Values for Tom Swift Jr. Books

Format I.	$3.00-$30.00	Format IV.	$1.00-$15.00
Format II.	$3.00-$25.00	Format V.	$1.00-$22.00
Volume 18	$4.00-$40.00	Slipcase Set	$60.00-$130.00
Format III.	$2.00-$16.00		
Volumes 29, 30	$5.00-$45.00		
Volume 31	$5.00-$75.00+		
Volume 32	$5.00-$100.00+		
Volume 33	$5.00-$200.00+		

Year	Volume	Pages
1954	**1. Tom Swift® and His Flying Lab**	208
1954	**2. Tom Swift® and His Jetmarine**	208
1954	**3. Tom Swift® and His Rocket Ship**	208
1954	**4. Tom Swift® and His Giant Robot**	211
1954	**5. Tom Swift® and His Atomic Earth Blaster**	210
1955	**6. Tom Swift® and His Outpost in Space**	210

Tom Swift Jr. 1 - 2 - 3

1. DJ/PC.

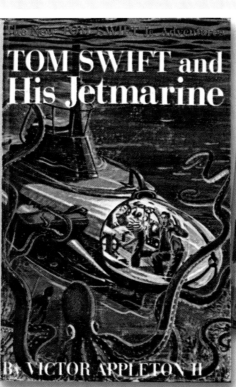

2. DJ/PC.

3. DJ/PC.

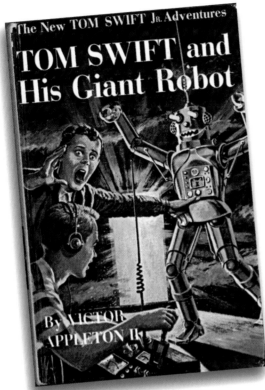

4. DJ/PC.

5. DJ/PC.

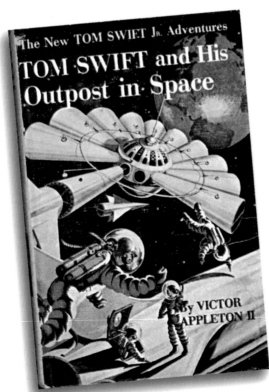

6. DJ/PC.

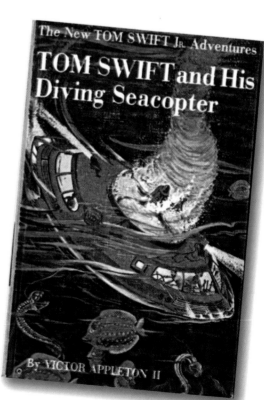

7. DJ/PC.

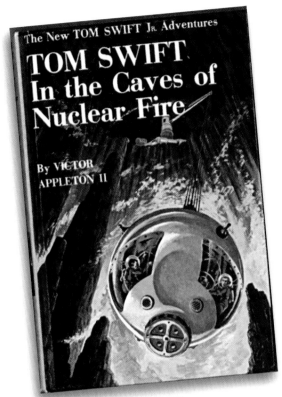

8. DJ/PC.

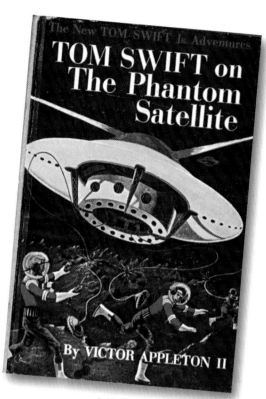

9. DJ/PC.

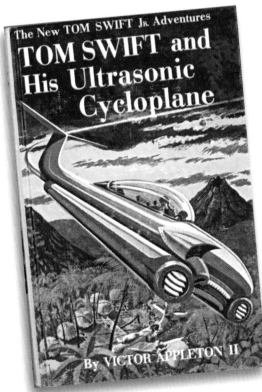

10. DJ/PC.

11. DJ/PC.

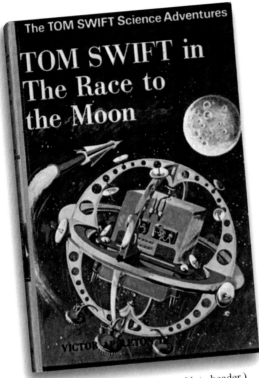

12. DJ/PC. (Collins Edition. Note header.)

13. DJ/PC.

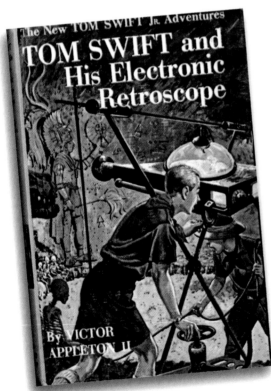

14. DJ/PC.

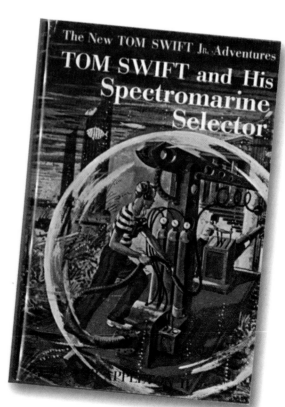

15. DJ/PC.

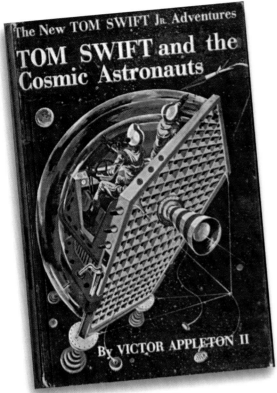

16. DJ/PC.

17. DJ/PC.

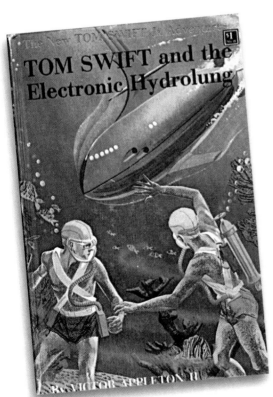

18. PC. (Format II.)

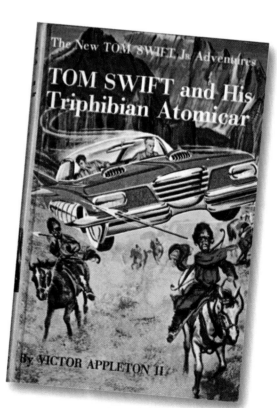

19. PC.

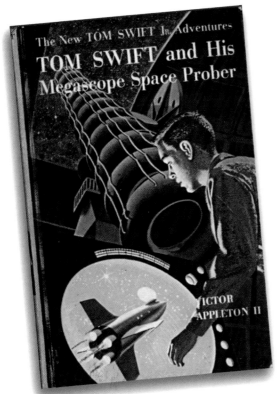

20. PC.

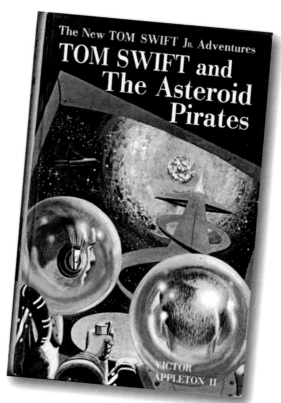

21. PC.

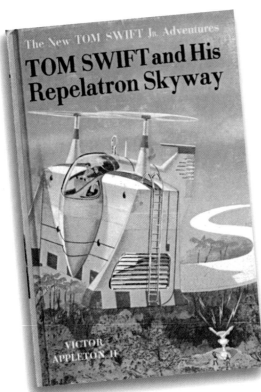

22. PC.

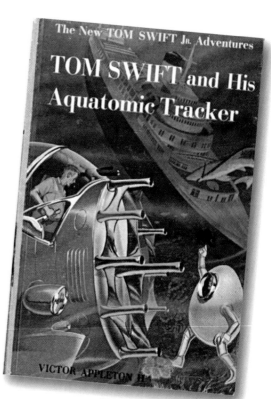

23. PC.

Tom Swift Jr. 24 - 25 - 26 - 27 - 28

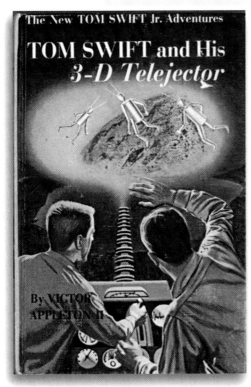

24. PC.

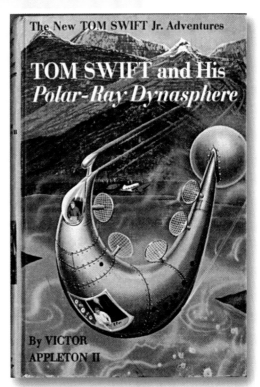

25. PC.

26. PC.

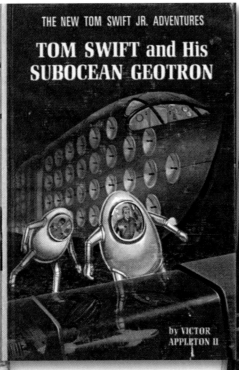

27. PC.

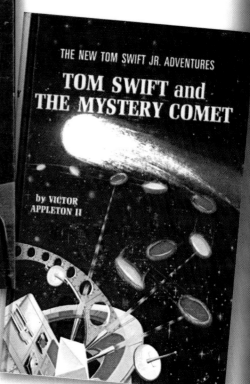

28. PC.

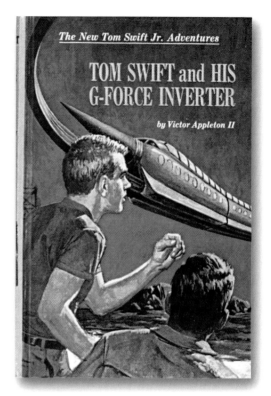

29. PC.

30. PC. *Sharon Kissell Collection.*

31. PC.

32. PC. *Sharon Kissell Collection.*

33. PC. *Sharon Kissell Collection.*

Tempo Digest-Size Paperback		
Year	Volume	Pages
1972	1. Tom Swift® in the Jungle of the Mayas	184
1972	2. Tom Swift® and the City of Gold	184
1972	3. Tom Swift® and the Cosmic Astronauts	184
1972	4. Tom Swift® and the Visitor from Planet X	184

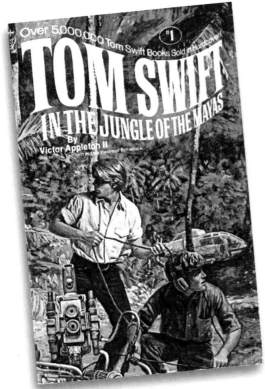

#1.

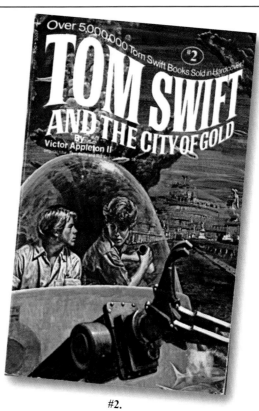

#2.

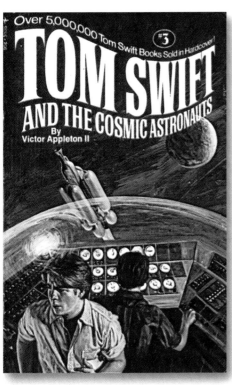

#3.

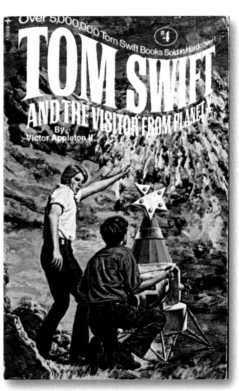

#4.

Tempo Mass-Market Paperback		
Year	Volume	Pages
1977	**1. Tom Swift® and His Flying Lab**	208
1977	**2. Tom Swift® and His Jetmarine**	208
1977	**3. Tom Swift® and His Rocket Ship**	208
1977	**4. Tom Swift® and His Giant Robot**	211
1977	**5. Tom Swift® and His Sky Wheel**	210
1977	**6. Tom Swift® in the Caves of Nuclear Fire**	214

Tempo 1977 paperback
set of Tom Swift®
books in slipcase.

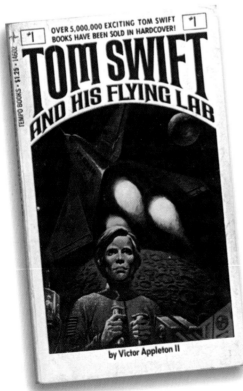

#1.

#2.

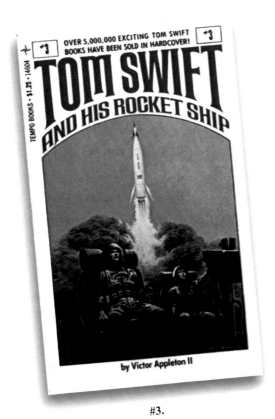

#3.

#4.

#5.

#6.

Tom Swift® - Third Series

When the Stratemeyer Syndicate took their juvenile series books to Simon & Schuster in 1979, the new titles from that company were published mostly as paperback books. Tom Swift® was revived in this format for a third series, beginning in 1981. The third series has eleven books and they are all credited to Victor Appleton. In these adventures Tom develops his inventions to further America's exploration of outer space. Tom and his friends travel to strange planets and far off galaxies.

This paperback set was published by a Simon & Schuster division called Wanderer. The first nine books were also printed with hard covers and dust jackets for libraries. The most notable thing about the Tom Swift® III books is that they have beautiful artwork on the covers.

Values for Tom Swift® III Books

Hard cover editions (Volumes 1 to 9) $3.00-$18.00
Paperback editions (Volumes 1 to 11) $3.00-$18.00

Tom Swift® III – Wanderer Editions			
Year	Volume	Year	Volume
1981	**1. The City In The Stars**	1983	**8. Crater of Mystery**
1981	**2. Terror On The Moons Of Jupiter**	1983	**9. Gateway To Doom**
1981	**3. The Alien Probe**	1983	**10. The Invisible Force**
1981	**4. The War In Outer Space**	1984	**11. Planet of Nightmares**
1981	**5. The Astral Fortress**		
1981	**6. The Rescue Mission**	Note: The above titles have initial capital letters as shown.	
1982	**7. Ark Two**		

Tom Swift® - Fourth Series

The third and fourth series of Tom Swift® books are called Tom Swift® III and Tom Swift® IV as collector designations. Simon & Schuster did not use these titles.

For the Tom Swift® IV paperback books, Simon & Schuster used the Archway division of the company for publication. There are thirteen books in the series. This set also has beautiful cover illustrations. By 1991, when the books were first printed, they cost $3.99 each, which still keeps them in line with a 50-cent hardback book of the 1930s, considering inflation over the years. In this thirteen-volume series, Tom Swift®, the resourceful inventor, experiences such challenges as combating evil forces who attempt world conquest, stopping vicious kickboxers from using technology for malevolent purposes, thwarting biologists whose experiments run rampant over humanity, and aiding NASA in excursions to the moon. Victor Appleton is the author of the books.

Values for Tom Swift® IV Books

Paperback books $3.00-$15.00

#7.

Tom Swift® IV – Archway Editions			
Year	**Volume**	**Year**	**Volume**
1991	1. The Black Dragon	1992	8. The Microbots
1991	2. The Negative Zone	1992	9. Fire Biker
1991	3. Cyborg Kickboxer	1992	10. Mind Games
1991	4. The DNA Disaster	1992	11. Mutant Beach
1991	5. Monster Machine	1993	12. Death Quake
1991	6. Aquatech Warriors	1993	13. Quantum Force
1992	7. Moon Stalker		

Tom Swift® - Fifth Series

The fifth set of Tom Swift® books is the most unusual of all, although there are only two books in the series. The title of the series is Hardy Boys® and Tom Swift® Ultra Thriller. The author is listed as Franklin W. Dixon, the credited writer of the Hardy Boys® books. The two paperback books also tell about more acquisitions of Simon & Schuster: They are Archway Paperbacks, published by Pocket Books, a division of Simon & Schuster, Inc., as were the books of the Tom Swift® IV series.

In the first book, *Time Bomb,* Tom Swift® and Frank and Joe Hardy join forces to stop a thug who is attempting to control time travel so that he can end the world. The other book is *The Alien Factor*, in which Tom, Frank and Joe offer aid to a beautiful girl from another planet in spite of all the dangers this may cause. The books have 215 and 219 pages, respectively, and beautifully detailed cover artwork.

Values for Tom Swift® V Books

Paperback books $3.00-$20.00

Tom Swift® V – Archway Editions	
Year	**Volume**
1992	1. Time Bomb
1993	2. The Alien Factor

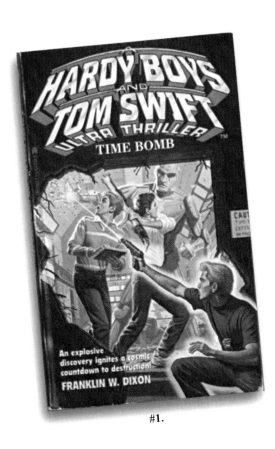

#1.

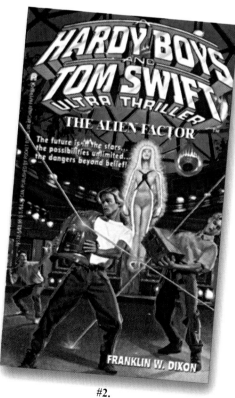

#2.

Two other popular boys' series of the mid-20th century that also have a scientific basis are the Rick Brant Science-Adventure books and Tom Corbett Space Cadet. Rick Brant was one of many new series that Grosset & Dunlap developed after World War II; Tom Corbett came about because of a popular program about space exploration on television in the early 1950s.

Rick Brant Science - Adventure Stories

The dust jackets of Rick Brant volumes 1 though 4 and 6 and all book fronts of dust-jacketed editions (volumes 1 though 16) call the series A Rick Brant Electronic Adventure. Volumes 5 and 7 through 16 called the series A Rick Brant Science-Adventure Story, as do the picture cover books volumes 17 through 24. Rick Brant and his friend Scotty live on Spindrift Island, off the coast of New Jersey, where Rick's father leads a team of electronic scientists. Rick and Scotty's adventures and the mysteries they solve involve science and electronics, at which the boys are experts.

The dust jackets and picture covers of the books show exciting action scenes, some of them involving violence. Many of the books relate to oceanographic problems and others include mysteries from space, such as flying saucers.

The author of the Rick Brant books is listed as John Blaine. The first three books of the series were co-written by Peter Harkins and Harold L. Goodwin; Goodwin did all the rest of them. The publisher, Grosset & Dunlap, cancelled the series in 1968 with volume 23. In 1989 because of fan demand, Goodwin had volume 24, *The Magic Talisman*, which he had completed more than twenty years earlier, printed by Manuscript Press of Tennessee. Volume 22 was reprinted by "Mystery and Adventure Series Review" because of the scarcity of the original edition. These two editions are picture cover books that are similar to the Grosset & Dunlap books. There is also a book by Grosset & Dunlap from 1960 that is larger in format than the twenty-three books of the series, called *Rick Brant's Science Projects*, a non-fiction work with a wrap dust jacket.

Rick Brant Book Formats

Grosset & Dunlap

I. 1947 – 1961
#1 – #16, including first printings of #1 – #16
Composition binding – first printings, #1 – #4 are rust colored; first printings, #5 – #7 are red; first printings, #8 – #16 are reddish tweed
Wrap dj; plain frontis
EPS show blue and white map of Spindrift Island

II. 1962 – 1968
#1 – #23, including first printings #17 – #23
Gray spine picture cover
Plain frontis; black and white eps of Spindrift map

Mystery and Adventure Series Review

III. #22
Similar to Grosset & Dunlap picture cover

Manuscript Press

IV. 1989
#24
Similar to Grosset & Dunlap picture cover, although slightly taller

---

Values for Rick Brant Books

Format I.	#1 – #4	$2.00-$35.00
	#5 – #7	$3.00-$50.00
	#8 – #16	$3.00-$65.00
Format II.	#1 – #16	$3.00-$30.00
	#17 – #18	$3.00-$50.00
	#19	$4.00-$75.00
	#20	$5.00-$95.00
	#21	$5.00-$150.00+
	#22	$5.00-$200.00+
	#23	$5.00-$300.00+
Format III.	#22	?
Format IV.	#24	?

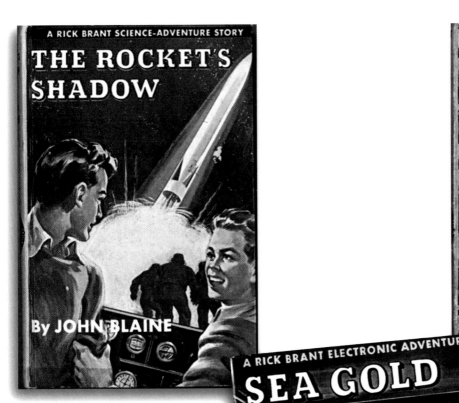

1. DJ/PC.

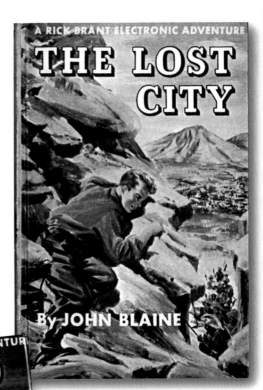

2. DJ/PC.

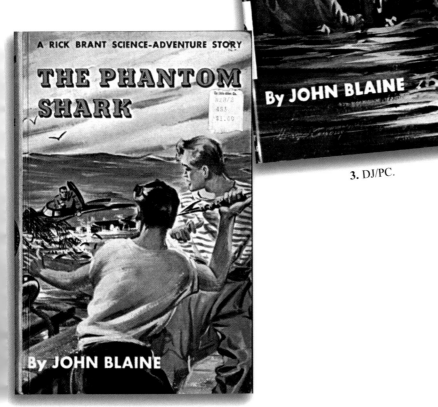

3. DJ/PC.

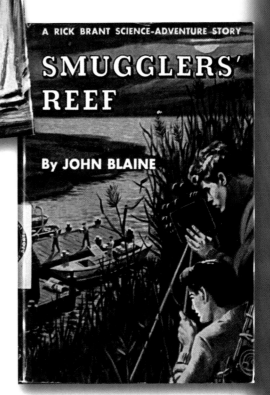

6. DJ/PC.

7. DJ/PC.

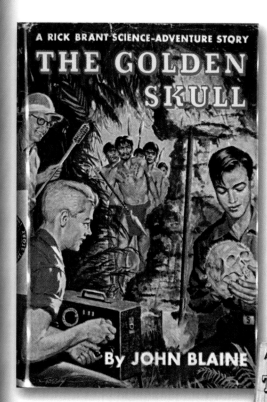

10. DJ/PC.

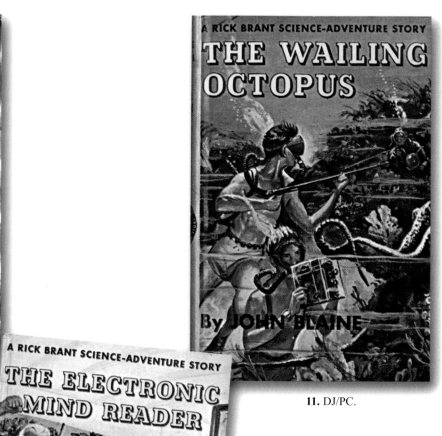

11. DJ/PC.

12. DJ/PC.

15. DJ/PC.

18. PC.

Year	Volume	Year	Volume
1947	1. The Rocket's Shadow	1958	13. The Scarlet Lake Mystery
1947	2. The Lost City	1958	14. The Pirates of Shan
1947	3. Sea Gold	1960	15. The Blue Ghost Mystery
1947	4. 100 Fathoms Under	1961	16. The Egyptian Cat Mystery
1948	5. The Whispering Box Mystery	1962	17. The Flaming Mountain
1949	6. The Phantom Shark	1963	18. The Flying Stingaree
1950	7. Smugglers' Reef	1964	19. The Ruby Ray Mystery
1951	8. The Caves of Fear	1965	20. The Veiled Raiders
1952	9. Stairway to Danger	1966	21. Rocket Jumper
1954	10. The Golden Skull	1967	22. The Deadly Dutchman
1956	11. The Wailing Octopus	1968	23. Danger Below!
1957	12. The Electronic Mind Reader	1989	24. The Magic Talisman

Tom Corbett Space Cadet

In 1950 the CBS Television Network conceived the series *Tom Corbet, Space Cadet* because of the popularity of the DuMont Network's show *Captain Video.* Tom Corbett was on for fifteen minutes a night on Monday, Wednesday and Friday from October to December 1950. Then from January 1951 to September 1952 it moved to ABC for the same amount of time on the same nights. Also during the summer of 1951 it was seen on Saturday evenings on NBC. From late 1952 until 1955 the show was on Saturday daytime. It was also an ABC radio show in 1952 with the same cast as the television program. Frankie Thomas played Tom Corbett, a cadet at Space Academy some 400 years in the future, and he was also one of the writers of the series. The novel *Space Cadet* by Robert A. Henley, first published by Scribners in 1948, was the basis of this children's television show. (First editions of the novel sell for more than $500.)

The eight-volume series Tom Corbett Space Cadet from Grosset & Dunlap was based on the television and radio series and had some of the same plot elements. Carey Rockwell, a Grosset & Dunlap "house name" is listed as the author of the Space Cadet Adventures. Willey Ley, an American rocket expert, was "Technical Adviser" for the books. Ley also helped to develop the Tom Corbett toy line. From 1952 to 1956 the Tom Corbett books were published with wrap dust jackets; in the 1960s they were printed again as picture cover books.

Large format push-out, or punch-out, book from Saalfield, 1952.

Tom Corbett Book Formats

Grosset & Dunlap

I. 1952 – 1956
#1 – #6, including first printings of #1 – #6
Blue tweed composition binding
Wrap dj; frontis and internal illustrations
Blue and white outer space scene eps

II. 1960s
#1 – #6
Picture cover book; wrap dj picture cover design
also over spine; pictures and eps as dj book

Values for Tom Corbet Books

Format I. $5.00-$50.00
Format II. $5.00-$25.00

Year	Volume	Pages
1952	1. Stand By for Mars!	216
1953	2. Danger in Deep Space	209
1953	3. On the Trail of Space Pirates	211
1953	4. The Space Pioneers	210
1954	5. The Revolt on Venus	213
1954	6. Treachery in Outer Space	210
1955	7. Sabotage in Space	212
1956	8. The Robot Rocket	181

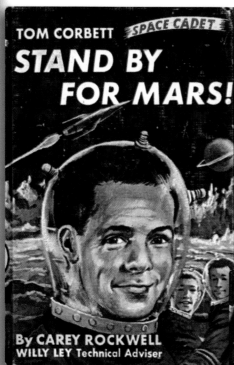

1. DJ/PC.

2. DJ/PC.

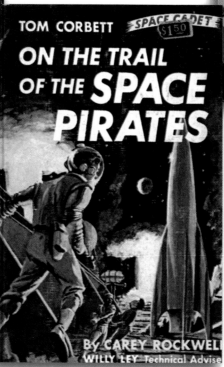

3. DJ/PC.

Chapter 4

"Approved by the Boy Scouts of America"

Percy Keese Fitzhugh

Though not quite as prolific as Edward Stratemeyer, Percy Keese Fitzhugh created an industry with his series books. Fitzhugh wrote many volumes of boys' books in several different series and used the pseudonym Hugh Lloyd for some of them. Fitzhugh was born in Brooklyn, New York, in 1876 and died in 1950. He lived and worked in Hackensack, New Jersey. All of his books are about young boys and most of them include the fact that they are Boy Scouts. Fitzhugh had eight series of boys' books, several books that were included in the series Buddy Books for Boys, and other boys' books that were not part of a series.

Fitzhugh's non-series books are *King Time* (H.M. Caldwell, 1908), *The Story of a Fight* (McLoughlin, 1907; authored as Hugh Lloyd), and *The Galleon Treasure* (Crowell, 1909). (Davis and Mattson, *A Collector's Guide to Hardcover Boys' Series Books*, page 467.)

Young Folks' Colonial Library

All six of these books are biographies of men involved in the American Revolutionary War. They are factual, but have dialogue added by Fitzhugh.

Young Folks' Colonial Library Format and Values

McLoughlin Brothers

These are small, short books with a color frontispiece and black and white illustrations. They are too rare to establish correct values for them.

Year	Volume
1906	1. The Story of John Paul Jones
1906	2. The Story of Ethan Allen, The Green Mountain Boy
1906	3. The Story of General Anthony Wayne
1906	4. The Story of General Richard Montgomery
1906	5. The Story of General DeKalb
1907	6. The Story of General Francis Marion

Tom Slade

Apparently the origin of this series was a motion picture, as the first book states, "Produced and Copyrighted by the Wedepict Motion Picture Corporation, Illustrations and Text used by special arrangement with the Boy Scouts of America, and approved and endorsed by them."

On the dust jackets of many volumes it says, "Approved by the Boy Scouts of America." The endpapers of the first book shows Police Commissioner Woods of New York and a Boy Scout troop in front of the Regent Theatre, where the first performance of "The Adventures of a Boy Scout" was shown. There are thirteen glossy photographs from the movie in the first book, which is titled *Tom Slade, Boy Scout of the Moving Pictures*.

The Tom Slade books have an unusual format in that the wrap-around dust jackets are black and white photographs of Boy Scouts in an outdoor setting that have been tinted in color and the end papers are photographs of boys in another action scene. These are different for each book. The glossy illustrations inside the books (after Volume 1) are paintings by artists, such as Walter S. Rogers.

The first Tom Slade book is a Horatio Alger-type story. Tom is a hoodlum from Barrel Alley who gradually becomes a highly respected First Class Scout. Later in the series Tom becomes a doughboy in France in World War I and when he returns home he is a scout leader at Temple Camp and a forest ranger. Tom also appears in other Fitzhugh books. In *Skinny McCord* he is a Boy Scout camp assistant.

Tom Slade Book Formats

Grosset & Dunlap

I. 1915 – 1917
    #1 – #3
    Tan or gray cloth binding
    Photographic eps, different for each book
    Volume 1 is *Tom Slade Boy Scout Of the Moving Pictures* and it has thirteen glossy photographs from the movie.
    Volumes 2 and 3 have a glossy frontis and three glossy internals by W.S. Rogers
    DJS are a colorized photograph with green bands at top and bottom of picture for titles

II. 1918 – 1930
    #1 – #19
    Green cloth binding
    Photographic eps, different for each book
    Volume 1 is *Tom Slade Boy Scout*

Glossy frontis and three to six glossy internals
DJS are a colorized photograph; Volume 19 eliminates green bands at top and bottom

III. 1930 – 1931
    #1, #2, #10, #11, #13, #15 – #19
    Titles now "*A Tom Slade Story: [former title]*"
    Book same Format II
    DJ has cream bands at top and bottom, instead of green

Whitman

IV. Circa 1940s
    #2304 *Tom Slade Boy Scout*
    #2305 *Tom Slade at Temple Camp*
    Composition binding with color dj
    (These are cheap reprints and are in tall and short versions)

Values for Tom Slade Books

Format I.	$2.00-$30.00
Format II.	
Volumes 1 – 17	$2.00-$30.00
Volume 18	$3.00-$40.00
Volume 19	$3.00-$55.00
Format III.	$3.00-$30.00
Format IV.	$2.00-$10.00

Year	Volume
1915	1. Tom Slade, Boy Scout [of the Moving Pictures]
1917	2. Tom Slade at Temple Camp
1917	3. Tom Slade on the River
1918	4. Tom Slade with the Colors
1918	5. Tom Slade on a Transport
1918	6. Tom Slade with the Boys Over There
1918	7. Tom Slade, Motor Cycle Dispatch Bearer
1919	8. Tom Slade with the Flying Corps
1920	9. Tom Slade at Black Lake
1921	10. Tom Slade on Mystery Trail
1922	11. Tom Slade's Double Dare
1923	12. Tom Slade on Overlook Mountain
1924	13. Tom Slade Picks a Winner
1925	14. Tom Slade at Bear Mountain
1926	15. Tom Slade, Forest Ranger

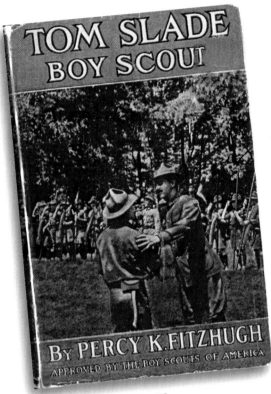

1. DJ.

2. DJ.

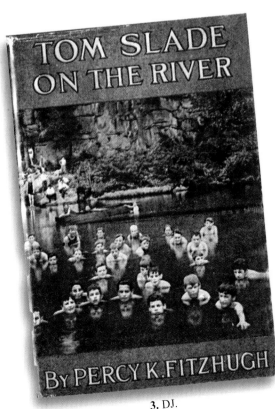

3. DJ.

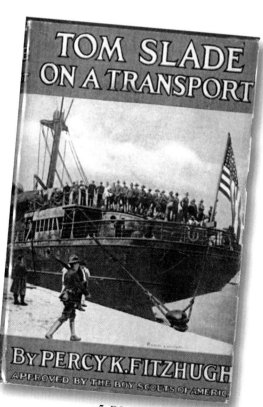

5. DJ.

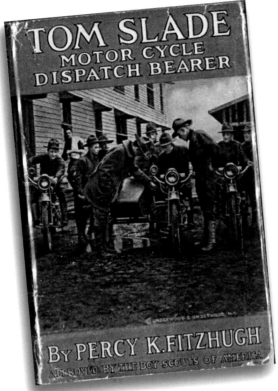

7. DJ.

12. DJ.

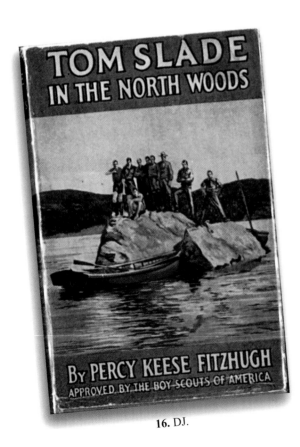

16. DJ.

7. DJ.

Roy Blakeley

The Roy Blakeley series is another Fitzhugh one that is "Approved by the Boy Scouts of America." The Roy Blakeley books are all done in a humorous vein and all are about Boy Scout adventures. Pee-Wee Harris and Westy Martin are also in these tales and they also take place at Temple Camp, like other Fitzhugh books.

Roy Blakeley Book Formats

Grosset & Dunlap

I. 1920 – 1922
#1 – #8
Gray cloth binding
Glossy frontis; three glossy or plain internals
(internals can be combinations of glossy
and/or plain)
Plain eps
All djs show colorized picture of Roy holding hat

II. 1923 – 1931
#1 – #18
Red cloth binding
Glossy frontis; three glossy internals
Plain eps
DJ same as Format I

Values for Roy Blakeley Books

Format I.	$3.00-$40.00
Format II.	$3.00-$40.00

Year	Volume
1920	1. Roy Blakeley
1920	2. Roy Blakeley's Adventures in Camp
1920	3. Roy Blakeley Pathfinder
1920	4. Roy Blakeley's Camp on Wheels
1920	5. Roy Blakeley's Silver Fox Patrol
1921	6. Roy Blakeley's Motor Caravan
1922	7. Roy Blakeley, Lost, Strayed or Stolen
1922	8. Roy Blakeley's Bee-Line Hike
1922	9. Roy Blakeley at the Haunted Camp
1923	10. Roy Blakeley's Funny-Bone Hike
1924	11. Roy Blakeley's Tangled Trails
1925	12. Roy Blakeley on the Mohawk Trail
1926	13. Roy Blakeley's Elastic Hike
1927	14. Roy Blakeley's Roundabout Hike
1928	15. Roy Blakeley's Happy-Go-Lucky Hike
1929	16. Roy Blakeley's Go-As-You-Please Hike
1930	17. Roy Blakeley's Wild Goose Chase
1931	18. Roy Blakeley Up In the Air

Pee-Wee Harris

The Pee-Wee Harris series, like Roy Blakeley, is a humorous one and also about Boy Scouts. Some of the same characters from Roy Blakeley and Tom Slade are in this series too, as well as adventures at Temple Camp.

Pee-Wee Harris Book Formats

Grosset & Dunlap

I. 1922 – 1930
#1 – #13
Tan cloth binding
Glossy frontis; three glossy internals
Plain eps
Color djs

Whitman

II. Circa 1940s
#2306 *Pee-Wee Harris* (#1)
#2307 *Pee-Wee Harris on the Trail* (#2)
Composition binding with color dj
(These are cheap reprints in tall and short versions)

Values for Pee-Wee Harris Books

Format I. $3.00-$40.00
Format II. $2.00-$12.00

Year	Volume
1922	**1. Pee-Wee Harris**
1922	**2. Pee-Wee Harris on the Trail**
1922	**3. Pee-Wee Harris in Camp**
1922	**4. Pee-Wee Harris in Luck**
1922	**5. Pee-Wee Harris Adrift**
1923	**6. Pee-Wee Harris F.O.B. Bridgeboro**
1924	**7. Pee-Wee Harris: Fixer**
1925	**8. Pee-Wee Harris As Good As His Word**
1926	**9. Pee-Wee Harris: Mayor For a Day**
1927	**10. Pee-Wee Harris and the Sunken Treasure**
1928	**11. Pee-Wee Harris on the Briny Deep**
1929	**12. Pee-Wee Harris in Darkest Africa**
1930	**13. Pee-Wee Harris Turns Detective**

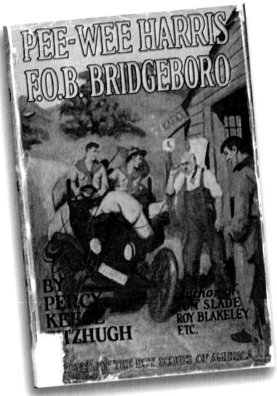

6. DJ.

5. DJ. Buddy Books For Boys.

Westy Martin

The Westy Martin series has the same characters as in the previously mentioned sets and Westy participates as a scout in Bridgeboro and at Temple Camp. A difference is that many of Westy's adventures take place in the American West, such as Yellowstone Park and the Rocky Mountains.

Westy Martin Book Formats

Grosset & Dunlap

I. 1924 – 1931
    #1 – #8
    Red cloth binding
    Glossy frontis; three glossy internals
    Plain eps
    Color pictorial djs

Note: In the early 1930s the first four Westy Martin books were bound together in one volume as *Out West With Westy Martin*. The dust jacket picture is from Volume 6.

Values for Westy Martin Books

Format I. $3.00-$40.00

Year	Volume
1924	1. Westy Martin
1924	2. Westy Martin in the Yellowstone
1925	3. Westy Martin in the Rockies
1926	4. Westy Martin on the Santa Fe Trail
1928	5. Westy Martin on the Old Indian Trail
1929	6. Westy Martin in the Land of Purple Sage
1930	7. Westy Martin on the Mississippi
1931	8. Westy Martin in the Sierras

Buddy Books For Boys

The series called Buddy Books For Boys was made up of various books from several different Grosset & Dunlap writers. Nine books by Percy Keese Fitzhugh are in the set. Five of them are about boys who appear in the other Boy Scout books, like Skinny McCord who is in some Pee-Wee Harris and Roy Blakeley books. Three of the Buddy Books by Ftizhugh are a small series about a Scout who flies. This is the Mark Gilmore series within a series. The three Mark Gilmore books were also in another series called Flying Stories. There is a total of twenty-eight Buddy Books For Boys by various Grosset & Dunlap writers, prominent among them Harold M. Sherman, who wrote many books on Sports and Adventures for Grosset & Dunlap. There are seven books in the Flying Stories series, with three by Fitzhugh, one by Sherman and three by Irving Crump.

Buddy Books For Boys Formats

Grosset & Dunlap

I. See dates at right
    #1 – #9
    Cloth binding, mostly green
    Glossy frontis; three glossy internals
    Plain eps
    Color djs

Values for Buddy Books For Boys by Fitzhugh

$2.00-$45.00

Year	Volume
1930	1. Lefty Leighton
1929	2. Spiffy Henshaw
1929	3. Wigwag Weigand
1927	4. Hervey Willetts
1928	5. Skinny McCord
1930	6. Mark Gilmore, Scout of the Air
1931	7. Mark Gilmore's Lucky Landing
1931	8. Mark Gilmore, Speed Flier
1930	9. The Story of Terrible Terry

Hal Keen and Skippy Dare by Hugh Lloyd

Hal Keen is a mystery series by Percy Keese Fitzhugh under a pseudonym. The ten books are from 1931 to 1934 and are about a red-headed detective. The Skippy Dare series of 1934 is three books about another young detective.

Hal Keen and Skippy Dare Book Formats

Grosset & Dunlap

Hal Keen:

I. 1931 – 1932
    #1 – #6
    Orange cloth binding
    Glossy frontis; four glossy internals
    Blank eps; color djs

II. 1932 – 1934
    #1 – #10
    Gray cloth binding
    Glossy frontis; four glossy internals
    Decorated eps
    Color djs

Whitman

III. Circa 1940s
     #2312 *The Hermit of Gordon's Creek* (#1)
     #2113 *Kidnapped in the Jungle* (#2)
     Composition binding with color dj
     (These are cheap reprints in tall and short
       versions)

Skippy Dare:

Grosset and Dunlap

I. 1934
    #1 – #3
    Red cloth binding
    Glossy frontis; decorated eps
    Color dj

Values for Hal Keen and Skippy Dare Books

These books are rare and seldom seen, even in the Whitman format.

Hal Keen

Year	Volume
1931	1. The Hermit of Gordon's Creek
1931	2. Kidnapped in the Jungle
1931	3. The Copperhead Trail Mystery
1931	4. The Smuggler's Secret
1931	5. The Mysterious Arab
1932	6. The Lonesome Swamp Mystery
1932	7. The Clue at Skeleton Rocks
1933	8. The Doom of Stark House
1933	9. The Lost Mine of the Amazon
1934	10. The Mystery at Dark Star Ranch

Skippy Dare

Year	Volume
1934	1. Among the River Pirates
1934	2. Held for Ransom
1934	3. Prisoners in Devil's Bog

Chapter 5

"Over the Ocean to Paris"

After Orville and Wilbur Wright of Dayton, Ohio, got a power-driven machine off the ground in Kitty Hawk, North Carolina, in December 1903, the topic of airplanes became a popular theme for boys' series books. There were quite a few boys' series about air travel in the early years of the 20th century. Some were The Airship Boys by H.L. Sayler in 1909, The Aeroplane Boys by Ashton Lamar in 1910, The Flying Boys by Edward S. Ellis in 1911, and Dave Dashaway from the Stratemeyer Syndicate (author Roy Rockwood) in 1913.

Nothing called attention to the possibilities of air travel like the solo flight that Charles Lindbergh made from New York to Paris in May 1927, including the use of planes in combat during World War I. Lindbergh and his plane, *The Spirit of St. Louis*, were among the most popular icons in America for many years after his historic transatlantic flight. Lindbergh inspired everyone. Stratemeyer's new series that capitalized on Lindbergh's adventures, the Ted Scott Flying Stories, began with three volumes that same year of 1927. The first one was, appropriately, *Over the Ocean to Paris*.

The Ted Scott stories concentrated on adventures that showed how valuable airplanes could be for the improvement of American life, such as carrying the mail. The four Bill Bolton Navy Aviator books came out in 1933. This series, by Lieutenant Noel Sainsbury, Jr., was about adventures in the air combined with solving mysteries, which should have caused it to become the most popular of the genre.

Because of the importance of pilots during World War I and World War II many boys' series books that related to air combat developed. Examples of these are The Air Combat Stories by Thomson Burtis and Eustace L. Adams in the 1930s; in the 1940s there was Al Avery's Yankee Flier and Canfield Cook's Lucky Terrell Flying Stories; and the Dave Dawson War Adventure Stories by Robert S. Bowen were printed from 1941 to 1946. All these series deal with aerial bombing and missions against "the enemy," popular themes during the emergencies of the world wars.

The heroes of the Aviation series books were far away in theme from Tom Swift® and his fantastic inventions in that life-threatening situations were common in them and that many elements of their plots were taken from the newspapers, giving them an immediate reality. They also show that successful boys' series books address contemporary situations.

Ted Scott Flying Stories

The first book in this series is *Over the Ocean to Paris or, Ted Scott's Daring Long Distance Flight*, published in 1927. The Ted Scott series is dedicated to Wilbur Wright, Orville Wright, Colonel Charles A. Lindbergh, Commander Richard E. Byrd, and other pioneers in flight. For years the Ted Scott books outsold the Hardy Boys® Mysteries, which also began in 1927. The titles of the Ted Scott books show how his adventures were similar to some of Lindbergh's early experiences with delivering airmail and flying around the country. Lindbergh was called "the

Lone Eagle." One of the Ted Scott books has this in the title – Volume 8, *The Lone Eagle of the Border*.

Various Stratemeyer Syndicate writers under the name Franklin W. Dixon, the "author" of the Hardy Boys® books, wrote the Ted Scott series. The early books have a red cover; the later volumes a tan one. All have glossy frontispieces. The Ted Scott books are noted for their high quality dust jacket pictures. Volumes 1 to 14 were done by Walter S. Rogers; Volumes 15 to 18 by J. Clemmens Gretta; and Volumes 19 and 20 by I.B. Hazelton.

```
┌─────────────────────────────────────────────────────────────┐
│              Ted Scott Flying Stories Formats                │
│                     Grosset & Dunlap                         │
│                                                              │
│      I.   1927 – 1932        │    II.  1933 – 1943           │
│           #1 – #15           │         #16 – #20             │
│           Red cloth binding  │         Tan cloth binding     │
│           Glossy frontis     │         Glossy frontis        │
│           Plain eps; color dj│         Decorated eps; color dj│
└─────────────────────────────────────────────────────────────┘
```

Values for Ted Scott Flying Stories

Format I. $2.00-$35.00
Format II. $2.00-$50.00

Year	Volume
1927	**1. Over the Ocean to Paris or, Ted Scott's Daring Long Distance Flight**
1927	**2. Rescued in the Clouds or, Ted Scott, Hero of the Air**
1927	**3. Over the Rockies with the Air Mail or, Ted Scott Lost in the Wilderness**
1928	**4. First Stop Honolulu or, Ted Scott Over the Pacific**
1928	**5. The Search for the Lost Flyers or, Ted Scott Over the West Indies**
1928	**6. South of the Rio Grande or, Ted Scott On a Secret Mission**
1928	**7. Across the Pacific or, Ted Scott's Hop to Australia**
1929	**8. The Lone Eagle of the Border or, Ted Scott and the Diamond Smugglers**
1929	**9. Flying Against Time or, Ted Scott Breaking the Ocean to Ocean Record**
1929	**10. Over the Jungle Trails or, Ted Scott and the Missing Explorers**
1930	**11. Lost At the South Pole or, Ted Scott in Blizzard Land**
1930	**12. Through the Air to Alaska or, Ted Scott's Search in Nugget Valley**
1930	**13. Flying to the Rescue or, Ted Scott and the Big Dirigible**
1931	**14. Danger Trails of the Sky or, Ted Scott's Great Mountain Climb**
1932	**15 Following the Sun Shadow or, Ted Scott and the Great Eclipse**
1933	**16. Battling the Wind or, Ted Scott Flying Around Cape Horn**
1934	**17. Brushing the Mountain Top or, Ted Scott Aiding the Lost Traveler**
1935	**18. Castaways of the Stratosphere or, Ted Scott Hunting the Vanished Balloonists**
1941	**19. Hunting the Sky Spies or, Testing the Invisible Plane**
1943	**20. The Pursuit Patrol or, Chasing the Platinum Pirates**

The Bill Bolton Naval Aviation Series

The Goldsmith Publishing Co. of Chicago was primarily a reprint house and the majority of its juvenile books are cheaply bound and printed on highly acidic paper. The four-volume Bill Bolton boys' series is an original printing, copyrighted by Goldsmith, and while the books are not the same quality as a Grosset & Dunlap book, they do have excellent dust jackets. The artist is J. Clemmens Gretta, who did many Ted Scott and Hardy Boys® for Grosset & Dunlap. Each Bill Bolton book has the same picture on the dust jacket though. An interesting feature of the Bill Bolton books is that they have such large print and wide spacing in them, which allows them to have the appearance and size of similar Grosset & Dunlap or Cupples & Leon books of the period.

Lieutenant Noel Sainsbury, Jr., a naval aviator of "the Great War," is the author of the Bill Bolton series. He also did the Great Ace Series and the Champion Sport Stories series for other publishers – Robert McBride & Co. and Cupples & Leon, respectively. On the dust jacket of *Bill Bolton and Winged Cartwheels* Sainsbury is quoted, "I shall never write war stories because I saw too much suffering during the war to wish to capitalize on it,

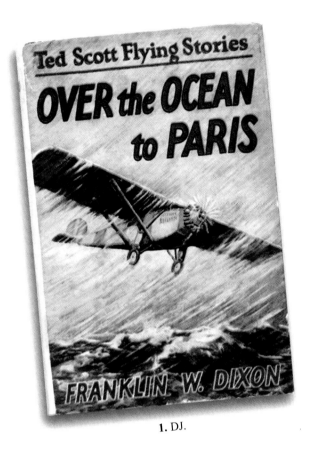

1. DJ.

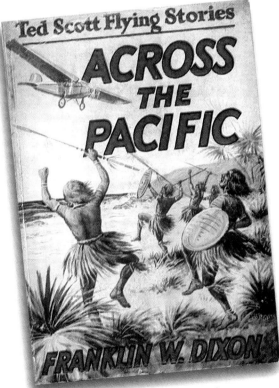

7. DJ. *Linda Burns Collection.*

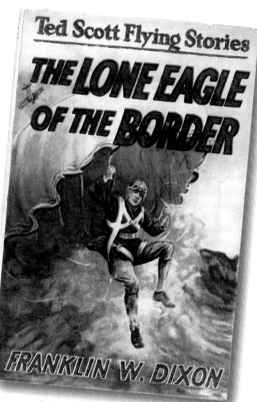

4. DJ.

8. DJ. *Linda Burns Collection.*

but most of the adventures by air, land and by sea depicted in this Bill Bolton Series actually occurred either during my travels or my term of war service."

Dorothy Wayne, the author of the Dorothy Dixon girls' series of the early 1930s, was the wife of Lieutenant Noel Sainsbury, Jr. In Wayne's Dorothy Dixon books, her boyfriend is Bill Bolton and he and other characters from the Bill Bolton series appear in the four Dorothy Dixon books. In *Dorothy Dixon Wins Her Wings*, Bill Bolton tells her that he knows Noel Sainsbury, his wife and his little girl. Dorothy Dixon informs Bill that she was named for Mrs. Sainsbury.

<table>
<tr><td>

Bill Bolton Naval Aviation Series Format

The Goldsmith Publishing Co.

I. 1933
#1 – #4
Cloth binding in various colors
No illustrations; plain eps
Dj in color by Gretta, same for each book

</td><td>

Values for Bill Bolton Naval Aviation Series

$1.50- $22.00

</td></tr>
</table>

Year	Volume
1933	**1. Bill Bolton, Flying Midshipman**
1933	**2. Bill Bolton and the Flying Fish**
1933	**3. Bill Bolton and the Hidden Danger**
1933	**4. Bill Bolton and the Winged Cartwheels**

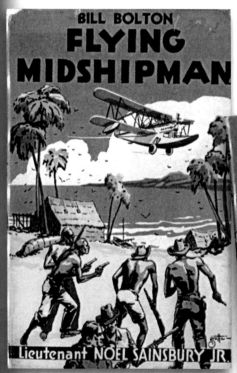

1. DJ.

4. DJ.

2. DJ from *Eagles of the Sky*, of the Sky Detectives Series from Goldsmith, by Ambrose Newcomb. This is a series of six tall books, 1930 to 1931.

Air Combat Stories for Boys

Because of the interest in air combat during World War II Grosset & Dunlap put together a set of sixteen boys' books by Thomson Burtis, Eustace Adams, and Al Avery (Rutherford G. Montgomery) and called the series Air Combat Stories for Boys. The first seven books in the series were first published in the 1930s and are about exploits in the air during World War I. The Yankee Flier portion of the series is about World War II. These books have spine numbers in the order as shown below.

Air Combat Stories for Boys Formats

Grosset & Dunlap

I. 1932
#1 – #4
Blue cloth binding
Glossy frontis; three glossy internals
Different color dj for each book

II. Mid-1930s
#1 – #5
Green cloth binding
#1 – #4, glossy frontis; three glossy internals
#5, glossy frontis; three plain internals
DJS as in Format I

III. 1940s
#1 – #16
Green cloth binding or composition binding
Glossy frontis or plain frontis
DJS as in Format I

Values for Air Combat Stories for Boys

Format I.	$2.00-$25.00
Format II.	$2.00-$25.00
Format III.	
Volumes 1 – 7	$3.00-$25.00
Volumes 8 – 12	$3.00-$30.00
Volumes 9 – 16	$3.00-$35.00

13. DJ.

16. DJ.

Year	Volume	Author
1932	1. Daredevils of the Air	Thomson Burtis
1932	2. Four Aces	Thomson Burtis
1932	3. Wing for Wing	Thomson Burtis
1932	4. Flying Blackbirds	Thomson Burtis
1935	5. Doomed Demons	Eustace L. Adams
1936	6. Wings of the Navy	Eustace L. Adams
1937	7. War Wings	Eustace L. Adams
1941	8. A Yankee Flier with the R.A.F.	Al Avery
1942	9. A Yankee Flier in the Far East	Al Avery
1943	10. A Yankee Flier in the South Pacific	Al Avery
1943	11. A Yankee Flier in North Africa	Al Avery
1944	12. A Yankee Flier in Italy	Al Avery
1944	13. A Yankee Flier Over Berlin	Al Avery
1945	14. A Yankee Flier in Normandy	Al Avery
1945	15. A Yankee Flier on a Rescue Mission	Al Avery
1946	16. A Yankee Flier Under Secret Orders	Al Avery

A Lucky Terrell Flying Story

This series is about "Lucky" Bob Terrell from Texas who joins the R.A.F. in England during World War II to bomb German planes. According to Grosset & Dunlap dust jacket blurbs, the author of the series, Canfield Cook, was a wartime flier himself. The eight Lucky Terrell books are the only series books that Cook wrote. These books have nice dust jackets and well-drawn frontispieces, but they are printed on "War Paper" and carry this notice on the title page.

Lucky Terrell Flying Stories Format

Grosset & Dunlap

I. 1942 – 1946
    #1 – #8
    Green composition binding
    Decorated eps; "War Paper"
    Plain frontis; color djs, different for each book

1. DJ.

Values for Lucky Terrell Books

#1 – #6	$1.00-$24.00
#7 – #8	$3.00-$45.00

Year	Volume
1942	1. Spitfire Pilot
1942	2. Sky Attack
1943	3. Secret Mission
1943	4. Lost Squadron
1943	5. Springboard to Tokyo
1944	6. Wings Over Japan
1945	7. The Flying Jet
1946	8. The Flying Wing

The War Adventure Series (Dave Dawson)

This series is also called Dave Dawson War Adventure Books. They are another indication of the tremendous patriotism and interest in combat during World War II. The titles of the books tell which theater of war was emphasized. Dave Dawson was another R.A.F. hero and like Lucky Terrell, he was originally from the United States, having been raised on Long Island. This series emphasizes action, fighting, and battles. The dust jacket blurbs tell that Dave and his English friend Freddy Farmer are involved in "true-to-fact adventures."

The ads on the back of the dust jackets tell that author R. Sidney Bowen was the youngest member of the Royal Flying Corps and the R.A.F. in World War I. He shot down a number of German planes and balloons and saw service in England, France, Belgium, Germany, Italy, Egypt, India, and British Somaliland. Bowen also held the World's Schoolboy Record for the 1000-yard run.

War Adventure Series Formats

Crown Publishers

I. 1940s
#1 – ?
Cloth bindings, various colors
No illustrations
Color dj, different for each volume

II. Late 1940s
#1 – ?
Composition bindings
No illustrations; dj same as in Format I

The Saalfield Publishing Company

III. Late 1940s
#1 – #15
Cloth bindings, various colors
Brittle "War Paper"
No illustrations
Color dj, different for each volume, same as in
    Format I

Values for War Adventure Series Books

Format I. and II.	Very rare
Format III.	$1.00-$15.00

Year	Volume
1941	**1. Dave Dawson at Dunkirk**
1941	**2. Dave Dawson with the R.A.F.**
1941	**3. Dave Dawson in Libya**
1941	**4. Dave Dawson on Convoy Patrol**
1942	**5. Dave Dawson at Singapore**
1942	**6. Dave Dawson, Flight Lieutenant**
1942	**7. Dave Dawson with the Pacific Fleet**
1942	**8. Dave Dawson with the Air Corps**
1942	**9. Dave Dawson with the Commandos**
1943	**10. Dave Dawson on the Russian Front**
1943	**11. Dave Dawson with the Flying Tigers**
1943	**12. Dave Dawson on Guadalcanal**
1944	**13. Dave Dawson at Casablanca**
1944	**14. Dave Dawson with the English Air Force**
1946	**15. Dave Dawson at Truk**

1. DJ.

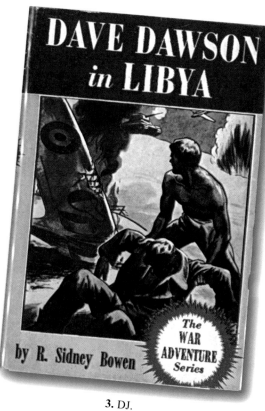

3. DJ.

Chapter 6

"On the Trail"

No genre of American fiction is more romantic and enduring as The Western. In former times "The West" was the American frontier – the area that was not settled by people of European background. In Colonial times this was fifty miles from the Atlantic coast. By the time of the Civil War it was roughly the western half of the United States, excluding the Pacific coast. This area of large ranches, wide-open ranges and cattle and wagon train trails is the setting for most of the literature and films about "The West." One of the most important historical theses in American history is Frederick Jackson Turner's "The Significance of the Frontier in American History" of 1893. Turner explained how the unique character of Americans and of the United States was caused by the moving frontier. There is no frontier in America now, but the romanticism and adventure associated with it still endures.

Many important American writers of fiction wrote novels of the frontier. One of the earliest was James Fenimore Cooper's "Leatherstocking Tales" of 1823 to 1841, when the Far West was upstate New York. Other important writers such as Mark Twain, Frank Norris, and Jack London wrote short stories of the Western tradition. Probably the most popular writer of Western fiction is Zane Grey, many of whose seventy-eight books were about the American West, including *Riders of the Purple Sage*, which has sold more than two million copies since it was first published in 1912. In recent times, the best known writer of Western fiction was Louis L'Amour, whose more than seventy books about the West have sold more than fifty million copies and are still in print.

The birth of the movies increased American and worldwide interest in the West. The first "real" American film, *The Great Train Robbery* (1903), was a Western. Countless movies about the West have been made, causing such "cowboys" as John Wayne, Roy Rogers, Gene Autry, and William "Hopalong Cassidy" Boyd to become famous all over the world. Even stars who were known for other genres of film, like Joan Crawford and Clark Gable, made Westerns. Some actors have won Academy Awards for roles in Western films. Examples are Warner Baxter for *In Old Arizona* in 1928, Gary Cooper in *High Noon* in 1951 and Clint Eastwood in *Unforgiven* in 1992. The year 1950 was the high point in the production of Western films. They made up thirty-four percent of the total of all films released.

Westerns were among the most popular television shows for many years, beginning with *The Lone Ranger* in 1949. By 1959 there were forty-eight television series that were Westerns. Some examples of these are *Bonanza, Cheyenne, Gunsmoke, Maverick, Rawhide, The Virginian,* and *Wagon Train*. From about 1955 until the early 1970s all the top-rated television programs were Westerns.

Although Westerns were prevalent as series books all during the 20th century they never achieved the success of other types, such as adventure stories, science-related themes, and series that concentrated on mysteries. The only explanation for this is that Edward Stratemeyer must not have been as interested in Westerns as other types of series books, although two Stratemeyer Syndicate series are among the top three in popularity. It is odd that there were not more Western series books, although there were several Roy Rogers and Gene Autry books for youngsters, as young boys were very interested in "cowboys and Indians" and in Western movies and television shows until recent times.

Number **18** of Buddy Books for Boys, Grosset & Dunlap, DJ, 1929.

From 1926 until 1942 there were twenty-one X Bar X Boys books. The boys, Roy and Teddy Manley, lived in "The West" on their father's ranch called the X Bar X. Like the coloring of the two Hardy Boys®, Roy had dark hair and eyes and Teddy had light hair and eyes. Their sister Belle turned thirteen in volume 4–*Big Bison Trail*. Roy and Teddy had interesting adventures and solved some mysteries from their western ranch. They lived during the time the stories were written–the 1920s and the 1930s–although ranch life dominated over contemporary issues.

Edward Stratemeyer developed the X Bar X Boys series in the mid-1920s, a time when the Syndicate began many new series, and listed the author as James Cody Ferris (See the Chart of Stratemeyer Syndicate books). The series is also called Western Stories For Boys. The earliest books are considered the best ones and they were written by Roger Garis, son of Howard Garis, from Edward Stratemeyer's outlines. Walter Karig, who wrote a few of the Nancy Drew® books, is credited with at least Volume 11 of the X Bar X Boys. An interesting note is that Leslie McFarlane, who wrote most of the early Hardy Boys® books, wrote a Volume 22 for the X Bar X Boys series, which was never printed.

The X Bar X Boys books are some of the Syndicate's most attractive, especially in the red format. All are "thick" volumes because of heavy paper. All have excellent artwork on the dust jackets. The artists of dust jackets and frontispieces of these books also did several Hardy Boys® books each. Volume 1 through 10 is by Walter S. Rogers, who painted covers for about 300 series books. J. Clemens Gretta did volumes 11 through 15. Gretta also designed the endpapers on the red-bound books. His most famous endpapers are the Hardy Boys® orange (or brown) ones. Paul Laune's illustrations enhanced the last six books–volumes 16 through 21.

X Bar X Boys Book Formats

Grosset & Dunlap

I. 1926 – 1932 #1 – #11 Gray cloth binding Plain eps; glossy frontis Color dj, different for each book	II. 1933 – 1942 #1 – #21 Red cloth binding Decorated eps #1 – #17 glossy frontis; #18 – -#21 plain frontis Color dj same as in Format I

4. DJ.

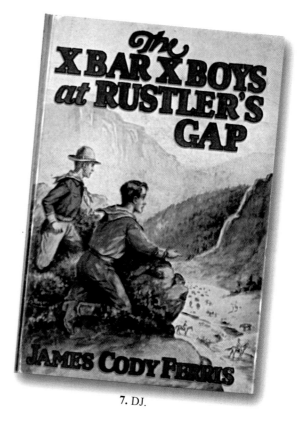

7. DJ.

Values for X Bar X Boys Books

Format I. $3.00-$35.00
Format II. $3.00-$45.00

Year	Volume
1926	1. The X Bar X Boys on the Ranch
1926	2. The X Bar X Boys in Thunder Canyon
1926	3. The X Bar X Boys on Whirlpool River
1927	4. The X Bar X Boys on Big Bison Trail
1927	5. The X Bar X Boys at the Round-Up
1928	6. The X Bar X Boys at Nugget Camp
1929	7. The X Bar X Boys at Rustlers' Gap
1929	8. The X Bar X Boys at Grizzly Pass
1930	9. The X Bar X Boys Lost in the Rockies
1931	10. The X Bar X Boys Riding for Life
1932	11. The X Bar X Boys in Smoky Valley
1933	12. The X Bar X Boys at Copperhead Gulch
1934	13. The X Bar X Boys Branding the Wild Herd
1935	14. The X Bar X Boys at the Strange Rodeo
1936	15. The X Bar X Boys with the Secret Rangers
1937	16. The X Bar X Boys Hunting the Prize Mustangs
1938	17. The X Bar X Boys at Triangle Mine
1939	18. The X Bar X Boys and the Sagebrush Mystery
1940	19. The X Bar X Boys in the Haunted Gully
1941	20. The X Bar X Boys Seek the Lost Troopers
1942	21. The X Bar X Boys Following the Stampede

The Lone Ranger

The Lone Ranger began as a radio series on January 30, 1933. Lone Ranger Television, a subsidiary of the Wrather Corporation, owns all rights to the Lone Ranger. In late 1932, radio station owner George W. Trendle knew that he needed a hit program to attract listeners to his Detroit station. He and his staff developed the idea of a western story about a masked "lone Texas ranger" and hired scriptwriter Fran Striker of Buffalo, New York, to fill in the details. Rossini's "William Tell Overture," used to introduce the show, became the best-known piece of classical music in the West. In the mid-1950s Trendle sold his Lone Ranger properties to Jack Wrather of the Wrather Corporation, which owned "Lassie," among other characters. The Lone Ranger television shows and movies from the 1950s featuring Clayton Moore were the most popular ones, although other actors played the part over the years.

Fran Striker (1903-1962), who also wrote *The Green Hornet* for radio, wrote the radio scripts, comic strips and books associated with the Lone Ranger and his Indian companion Tonto. The Lone Ranger was described as being just over six feet tall, good looking, and weighing about 190 pounds. He wore silver shoes, had silver bullets in his gun, and his horse was named Silver. The stories took place in the years following the American Civil War.

There are many other Lone Ranger books for children, apart from the series listed here. In the books, radio and television shows, and in the movies before 1981 the Lone Ranger and Tonto rounded up outlaws and helped to send criminals to prison. They did not shoot or kill anyone nor were they involved in violent situations in the books, all of which were meant for young readers. None of the television shows about the Lone Ranger were violent either. The only Lone Ranger story that employed violence and in which criminals were gunned down is the 1981 film *The Legend of the Lone Ranger*, which starred newcomers Klinton Spilsbury as the Lone Ranger and Michael Horse as Tonto. This movie was a critical and commercial failure in all respects. Spilsbury's voice was even dubbed in it.

The first volume of the Lone Ranger series from Grosset & Dunlap was written by Gaylord Dubois "based on the famous radio adventure series by Fran Striker."

Later editions of the first book were revised by Striker and carry his name on them. Striker wrote the rest of the books.

Striker also wrote the eight Tom Quest books published by Grosset & Dunlap. Paul Laune illustrated the first six Lone Ranger books and also did the decorated endpapers and glossy frontispieces for them.

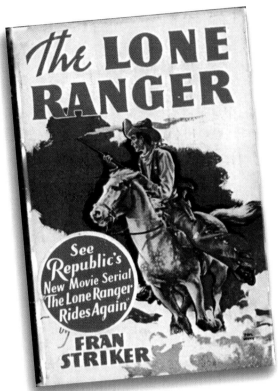

1. DJ.

The Lone Ranger Book Formats

Grosset & Dunlap

I.   1936 – 1950
      #1 – #12
      Tan cloth or tan composition binding
      #1 – #5, glossy frontis; #6 – #12 plain frontis
      Decorated eps
      Color dj, different for each book

II.   1951 – 1956
      #1 – #18
      Gray or tan composition binding
      Plain frontis or no frontis
      EPS and dj same as in Format I

Values for Lone Ranger Books

Format I. $3.00-$45.00
      (more if Gaylord Dubois on cover or title page)
Format II. $3.00-$40.00

Year	Volume
1936	1. The Lone Ranger
1938	2. The Lone Ranger and the Mystery Ranch
1939	3. The Lone Ranger and the Gold Robbery
1939	4. The Lone Ranger and the Outlaw Stronghold
1940	5. The Lone Ranger and Tonto
1941	6. The Lone Ranger at the Haunted Gulch
1941	7. The Lone Ranger Traps the Smugglers
1943	8. The Lone Ranger Rides Again
1946	9. The Lone Ranger Rides North
1948	10. The Lone Ranger and the Silver Bullet
1949	11. The Lone Ranger on Powder Horn Trail
1950	12. The Lone Ranger in Wild Horse Canyon
1951	13. The Lone Ranger West of Maverick Pass
1952	14. The Lone Ranger on Gunsight Mesa
1953	15. The Lone Ranger and the Bitter Spring Feud
1954	16. The Lone Ranger and the Code of the West
1955	17. The Lone Ranger: Trouble on the Santa Fe
1956	18. The Lone Ranger on Red Butte Trail

A Bret King Mystery

One of the last Stratemeyer Syndicate's new series was the Bret King Mysteries that began in 1960 and endured for nine volumes.

These stories took place in the modern West on Rimrock Ranch in New Mexico and featured eighteen-year-old Bret King, his sister Jinx, and his brother Rusty. The back of the dust jackets states, "[They are] stories of the great outdoors, written by one of America's most famous Western authors." The Stratemeyer Syndicate name for the author is Dan Scott. Arthur Svenson, a Syndicate associate, and others have been credited as the actual writers of the series.

Joe Beeler illustrated eight of the books. Santo Sorrentino did the art for Volume 4, which matches the other books in the set.

Bret King Book Formats

Grosset & Dunlap

I. 1960 – circa 1962
    #1 – #7 ?
    Gray textured composition binding
    Plain frontis and internal illustrations
    Decorated eps
    Wrap color dj, different for each volume

II. Circa 1962 – 1964
     #1 – #9
     Picture cover that matches the dj books
     Insides as in Format I

Values for Bret King Books

Format I.	$2.00-$20.00
Format II.	$2.00-$16.00

Year	Volume	Year	Volume
1960	1. The Mystery of Ghost Canyon	1961	6. The Secret of Fort Pioneer
1960	2. The Secret at Hermit's Peak	1962	7. The Mystery of the Comanche Caves
1960	3. The Range Rodeo Mystery	1963	8. The Phantom of Wolf Creek
1960	4. The Mystery of Rawhide Gap	1964	9. The Mystery of Bandit Gulch
1960	5. The Mystery at Blizzard Mesa		

2. DJ.

3. DJ.

4. DJ.

Chapter 7

Comic Series

There were not many boys' series books that were deliberately humorous, although the ones that were had tremendous popularity.

Some of the series of Percy Keese Fitzhugh, such as Roy Blakeley and Pee-Wee Harris concentrated on humor, but probably the most popular of all series books with comical characters in them are those by Leo Edwards. Collectors eagerly seek Edwards' Andy Blake, Jerry Todd, and Poppy Ott books today. Another humorist whose books were quite successful and which have a large following is Clarence Budington Kelland, best known among series books collectors for his clever fat boy Mark Tidd.

Leo Edwards

Leo Edwards is the pen name of Edward Edson Lee, who was born September 2, 1884, near Streator, Illinois. Grosset & Dunlap published thirty-nine Leo Edwards books in five series – Andy Blake (four books), Jerry Todd (sixteen books), Poppy Ott (eleven books), Trigger Berg (four books), and Tuffy Bean (four books).

Mr. Lee began his working career in Beloit, Wisconsin, in the advertising department of the P.B. Yates Machine Company in 1910. He was at the Burroughs Adding Machine Company in Detroit, Michigan, from 1915 to 1917, when he became advertising manager of the Autocall Company in Shelby, Ohio. By 1920 he was writing stories

for boys, which were published in the local Shelby newspaper and later in *Boys' Magazine*. Based on the initial success of his stories, Lee returned to Wisconsin, where he wrote his books for boys under the name Leo Edwards. He died on September 28, 1944.

Edwards' humorous books required unique illustrations to point out their comical aspect. The most important illustrator of his work was Bert Salg (1881-1938), who became a Grosset & Dunlap illustrator in 1921. Salg did the first eight Poppy Ott books, the first thirteen Jerry Todd books, and all of the Andy Blake, Trigger Berg, and Tuffy Bean books for Grosset & Dunlap.

This photograph was taken near the home of Leo Edwards (Edward Edson Lee) on Lake Ripley, in Cambridge, Wisconsin, in the late 1930s. The little guy standing at the table at Edwards' left is Jerry Olson. The tall guy in the striped shirt at the far right is Donny Rumpf, a friend of Jerry Olson, to whom Edwards dedicated *Jerry Todd's Up-the-Ladder Club*. This photograph originally appeared in *The Cambridge News. Courtesy of Jerry Olson.*

Andy Blake Books

Andy Blake was a young businessman in advertising. Appleton initially published the first book in 1921 as *Andy Blake in Advertising*. Grosset & Dunlap issued it simply as *Andy Blake* in 1928.

2. DJ. *Jim Towey Collection.*

Andy Blake Book Format

Grosset & Dunlap

1928 – 1930
#1 – #4
Red cloth binding
Glossy frontis; three glossy internals
Color djs, different for each book

Andy Blake Book Values

$6.00-$80.00+

Year	Volume
1928	**1. Andy Blake**
1928	**2. Andy Blake's Comet Coaster**
1929	**3. Andy Blake's Secret Service**
1930	**4. Andy Blake and the Pot of Gold**

Jerry Todd Series

The Jerry Todd series is probably Leo Edwards' most popular one of all. The sixteen books are mystery tales in a humorous vein. The titles listed show this well. Jerry and his pals Poppy, Red, Scoop, Al, Peg, Slats, and Tail Light have many adventures in their hometown of Tutter.

Jerry Todd Book Formats

Grosset & Dunlap

I. 1924 – 1932
#1 – #11
Red cloth binding
Glossy frontis; three glossy internals
Plain eps; color djs, different for each volume

II. 1934 – 1940
#1 – #16
Red cloth binding, with picture of a goldfish
wearing a top hat
#1 – #13 glossy frontis; three glossy internals

#14 – #15 plain frontis; three plain internals
Illustrated eps show map of Tutter
DJ, same as Format I

III. 1940+
#1 – #16
Red cloth binding (plain)
Plain frontis
DJ and so forth same as Format I

Jerry Todd Book Values

All formats $8.00-$85.00+

Year	Volume
1924	1. Jerry Todd and the Whispering Mummy
1924	2. Jerry Todd and the Rose-Colored Cat
1925	3. Jerry Todd and the Oak Island Treasure
1925	4. Jerry Todd and the Waltzing Hen
1925	5. Jerry Todd and the Talking Frog
1926	6. Jerry Todd and the Purring Egg
1927	7. Jerry Todd in the Whispering Cave
1928	8. Jerry Todd: Pirate
1929	9. Jerry Todd and the Bob-Tailed Elephant
1930	10. Jerry Todd, Editor-in-Grief
1932	11. Jerry Todd, Caveman
1934	12. Jerry Todd and the Flying Flapdoodle
1936	13. Jerry Todd and the Buffalo Bill Bathtub
1937	14. Jerry Todd's Up-the-Ladder Club
1938	15. Jerry Todd's Poodle Parlor
1940	16. Jerry Todd's Cuckoo Camp

3. DJ. *Sharon Kissell Collection.*   **5.** DJ. *Jim Towey Collection.*

10. DJ. *Jim Towey Collection.*

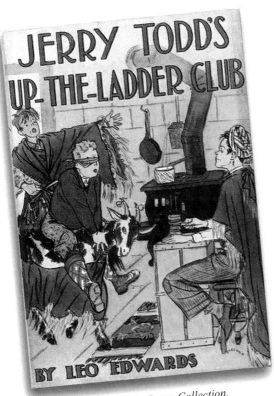

14. DJ. *Linda Burns Collection.*

15. DJ. *Jim Towey Collection.*

Poppy Ott Series

The Poppy Ott books are a mystery-adventure series written in a humorous style about Jerry Todd's bosom chum and other boys. Poppy Ott is the "Juvenile Jupiter Detective."

Poppy Ott Book Formats

Grosset & Dunlap

I. 1926 – 1930
#1 – #7
Red cloth binding
Glossy frontis; three glossy internals
Plain eps
Color dj, different for each volume

II. 1930 – 1937
#1 – #9
Red cloth binding with picture of goldfish in top hat on front
Glossy frontis; three glossy internals
Eps show a parade
Color dj as in Format I

III. 1938 – 1940+
#1 – #11
Red cloth binding without picture
Glossy frontis
#10 – #11 have different eps than Format II
#10 – #11 have wrap color djs

Note: Volume 10 and 11 were called The Poppy Ott Detective Stories.

Poppy Ott Book Values

All formats $8.00-$85.00+

Year	Volume
1926	1. Poppy Ott and the Stuttering Parrot
1926	2. Poppy Ott's Seven League Stilts
1927	3. Poppy Ott and the Galloping Snail
1927	4. Poppy Ott's Pedigreed Pickles
1928	5. Poppy Ott and the Freckled Goldfish
1928	6. Poppy Ott and the Tittering Totem
1930	7. Poppy Ott and the Prancing Pancake
1933	8. Poppy Ott Hits the Trail
1937	9. Poppy Ott and Co., Inferior Decorators
1938	10. The Monkey's Paw
1939	11. The Hidden Dwarf

Trigger Berg Stories

Trigger Berg and his pals were younger boys than Jerry Todd and Poppy Ott and the books were meant for younger readers. Other chaps in the stories are Friday, Slats, and Tail Light.

Trigger Berg Book Formats

Grosset & Dunlap

I. 1930 – 1931
#1 - #3
Red cloth binding
Glossy frontis and three glossy internals
Plain eps
Color dj, different for each book

II. 1933+
#1 – #4
Red cloth binding with picture of a goldfish in top hat on front
Glossy frontis and three glossy internals
Color eps of boys at clubhouse meeting

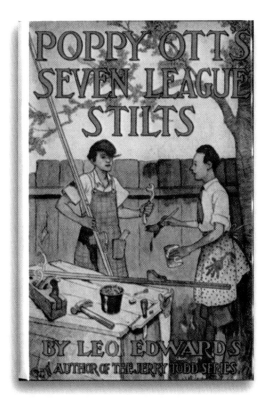

2. DJ. *Jim Towey Collection.*

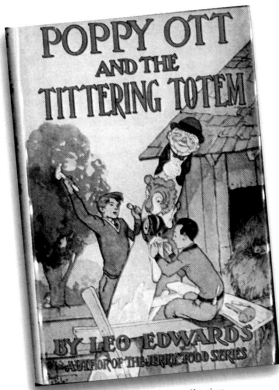

6. DJ. *Jim Towey Collection.*

10. DJ. *Jim Towey Collection.*

Trigger Berg Book Values

All formats $6.00-$40.00

Year	Volume
1930	**1. Trigger Berg and the Treasure Tree**
1930	**2. Trigger Berg and His 700 Mousetraps**
1931	**3. Trigger Berg and the Sacred Pig**
1933	**4. Trigger Berg and the Cockeyed Ghost**

Tuffy Beans Series

Tuffy is a funny little lost dog that narrates his own stories. He tells about his brother Cobby and also about their acquaintances Cocky Beans, Wiggles, Mutt, and others who have hilarious adventures.

Tuffy Beans Book Formats

Grosset & Dunlap

I.   1931
#1 – #3
Red cloth binding
Plain eps
Glossy frontis; many plain internals
Color dj, different for each book

II. 1932
#1 – #4
Red cloth binding with picture of a goldfish in a top hat on front
Illustrations as in Format I
Decorated eps with scenes of Tuffy
Color dj as in Format I

Tuffy Beans Book Values

All Formats $4.00-$45.00

Year	Volume
1931	**1. Tuffy Bean's Puppy Days**
1931	**2. Tuffy Bean's One-Ring Circus**
1931	**3. Tuffy Bean at Funny Bone Farm**
1932	**4. Tuffy Bean and the Lost Fortune**

2. DJ. *Jim Towey Collection.*

1. DJ. *Jim Towey Collection.*

Mark Tidd

The Mark Tidd series by Clarence Budington Kelland (1881-1964) is only nine books but as they were published from 1913 through the 1940s there are many different printings and formats. Harper & Brothers originally published this series from 1913 to the early 1930s. In 1934 Grosset & Dunlap acquired the reprint rights to the series and printed the books until the time of World War II.

Clarence Budington Kelland's first published book was *Mark Tidd: His Adventures and Strategies* in 1913. Kelland also wrote the juvenile series Catty Atkins, five books from 1920 to 1924, published by Harper & Brothers.

His many adult short stories and novels, such as *Mr. Deeds Goes to Town*, which was made into a movie with Gary Cooper in 1936, and the series of more than 100 short stories about "Scatergood Bains," which was in the *Saturday Evening Post* and *American Magazine*, were very popular in their time. Kelland was editor of the magazine *American Boy* (1907-1915), which published many of his Mark Tidd stories, including "Mark Tidd Back Home" in 1931, which completed the saga of this character.

Mark Tidd is an unusual juvenile series hero in that he is very fat and he stutters when he speaks. The books tell of the adventures, dangers, and mysteries in which Mark and his friends Tallow, Binney, and Plunk are involved. The Mark Tidd novels have a great deal of humor in them, usually provided by adults who are trying to thwart and outwit the boys. The names of characters in the books, such as Tecumseh Androcles Spat, and the use of unusual wording, such as "calc'late" to mean "intend to " or "think that" adds to the comic elements. The first six books take place in Wicksville, Michigan; the last three are set in Europe and the Near East.

The Mark Tidd books were attractively produced. In the 1920s Harper & Brothers bound them in colorful hard covers with an appliqué picture on front. There were several different Harper & Brothers covers and dust jackets used over the years. The Grosset & Dunlap reprints are notable for their colorful endpapers that matched the dust jackets. From both publishers, all are "thick" books. The Harper & Brothers editions have as many as eight glossy illustrations in them; the Grosset & Dunlap versions have only a frontispiece. The illustrators of internals were W.W. Clarke for Volumes 1 to 6 and 8; F.C. Yohn for Volume 7; and T. Victor Hall for Volume 9.

Mark Tidd Book Formats

Harper & Brothers

I. 1913 – circa 1920
#1 – #6
Cloth binding, various colors, line-drawn picture printed in one or two colors
Decorated or plain eps; glossy frontis
#1, #3, and #5 have seven glossy internals; #2 and #4 have six; #6 has four
DJ on white background with same picture as cover

II. 1920s
#1 – #6
Cloth binding, various colors with full-size appliqué picture or small one at top (these are usually two-color pictures)
Decorated or plain eps
Glossy frontis; glossy internals as Format I or three glossy internals each
DJ with same picture as appliqué front cover

III. Late 1920s – early 1930s
#1 – #9
Cloth binding in red, tan, green, blue, maroon, orange, or other color with narrow appliqué color picture of Mark Tidd or appliqué picture of boys; also line-drawn covers with one or two colors
Glossy frontis; three glossy internals
DJ of boys in scene, of which the appliqué cover is a part, or dj of scene from story for #7, #8, and #9

Note: There are also other combinations of all the above.

3. Harper & Brothers, Format I DJ.

5. Harper & Brothers, Format I DJ.

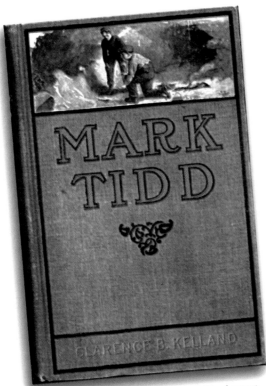

1. Harper & Brothers, Format II appliqué cover.

4. Harper & Brothers, Format II DJ.

1. Harper & Brothers, Format III appliqué cover.

6. Harper & Brothers, Format III appliqué cover.

7. Harper & Brothers, Format III, DJ B.

8. Harper & Brothers, Format III, DJ B.

9. Harper & Brothers, Format III, DJ B.

IV. 1934 – circa 1942
   #1 – #9
   Orange cloth or composition binding with black drawn head of Mark Tidd on front and spine.
   Color eps of boys in scene (sign painter one from Harper & Brothers' Books)
   Glossy frontis; four different scenic djs (same as the Harper & Brothers djs as in Format III);
      three form a single picture if matched

Note: The cloth boards are from the earlier Grosset & Dunlap years; composition ones from later print runs. These vary from a smooth surface to a quite pebbly looking one.

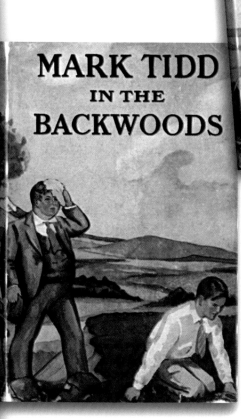

1. Grosset & Dunlap DJ, which is same as Harper & Brothers Format III with boys in scene.

2. Grosset & Dunlap DJ, which is same as Harper & Brothers Format III with boys in scene.

3. Grosset & Dunlap DJ; same as Harper & Brothers Format III with boys in scene.

5. Grosset & Dunlap DJ; same as Harper & Brothers Format III with boys in scene.

6. Grosset & Dunlap DJ; same as Harper & Brothers Format III with boys in scene.

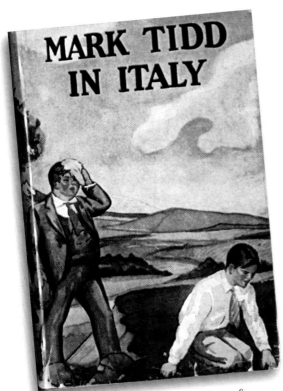

7. Grosset & Dunlap DJ; same as Harper & Brothers Format III with boys in scene.

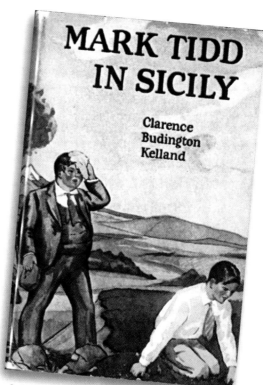

9. Grosset & Dunlap DJ; same as Harper & Brothers Format III with boys in scene.

How to tell the printing, or edition, of a Harper & Brothers Book

On the copyright page, there are letters, for example **G-H**.
The first letter refers to the month. **A** to **M** equals January to December.
The second letter is the year, taken from this chart:

M	1912	**U**	1920	**C**	1928
N	1913	**V**	1921	**D**	1929
O	1914	**W**	1922	**E**	1930
P	1915	**X**	1923	**F**	1931
Q	1916	**Y**	1924	**G**	1932
R	1917	**Z**	1925	**H**	1933
S	1918	**A**	1926	**I**	1934
T	1919	**B**	1927	**J**	1935

From the chart, the **G-H** on the copyright page tells the book was printed in July 1933. A book that has **I-R** on the copyright page was printed in September 1917. Many Harper & Brothers books that are first editions have this stated on the copyright page. Grosset & Dunlap reprints of Mark Tidd books carry the above letters on the copyright page also, but they have no meaning, other than that they were on the original Harper & Brothers plates from which the Grosset & Dunlap books were printed.

Values for Mark Tidd Books

Format I.	$10.00-$250.00+
Format II.	$9.00-$200.00+
Format III.	$8.00-$95.00
Format IV.	$6.00-$60.00

Year	Volume	Pages
1913	**1. Mark Tidd: His Adventures and Strategies**	317
1914	**2. Mark Tidd in the Backwoods**	281
1915	**3. Mark Tidd in Business**	271
1916	**4. Mark Tidd's Citadel**	280
1917	**5. Mark Tidd, Editor**	287
1918	**6. Mark Tidd, Manufacturer**	257
1925	**7. Mark Tidd in Italy**	264
1926	**8. Mark Tidd in Egypt**	237
1928	**9. Mark Tidd in Sicily**	208

Chapter 8

Sports Series

There are probably more series of boys' books about sports than any other genre, including mysteries and aviation. Boys' books about sports have been published since the early years of series books. In 1897 the Stratemeyer series Bound to Win featured sports stories, as did The Young Sportsmen series of the same year. Other Stratemeyer series, such as Dave Porter and The Rover Boys, had several volumes concerned with sports. The Baseball Joe series, fourteen books from 1912 to 1928, and the Garry Grayson Football Stories, ten books from 1926 to 1932, are other Stratemeyer series that were popular in their time.

Even Zane Grey, known for his adult Western books, had a little-known Grosset & Dunlap series, put together from earlier 20th century books, which featured sports. These are the ten books in the Zane Grey Books For Boys series that included three books about baseball. They are *The Redheaded Outfield*, *The Shortstop* and *The Young Pitcher*.

In the 1920s and 1930s Harold M. Sherman's Sports Stories were comprised of several short series about baseball, football, and basketball. Two other non-Stratemeyer series that endured into the 1960s featured the young athletes Chip Hilton and Bronc Burnett. Chip excelled at baseball, basketball and football. Bronc concentrated on baseball and football. All the sports series benefit from the fact that baseball, football and basketball games make good action scenes for paintings for dust jackets. The Chip Hilton series in particular has some of the best cover art of any Grosset & Dunlap boys' or girls' series books.

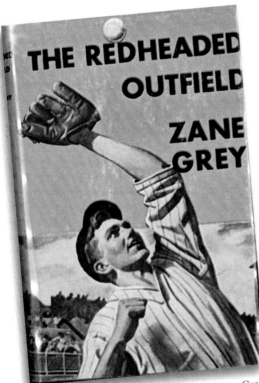

DJ from *The Redheaded Outfield* by Zane Grey from the Zane Grey Books for Boys Series, 1950s Grosset & Dunlap printing of this old-time series from the early 20th century.

DJ of *The Coach* by Arthur Stanwood Pier from the series Sports Stories by Arthur Stanwood Pier, David McKay Company, 1928.

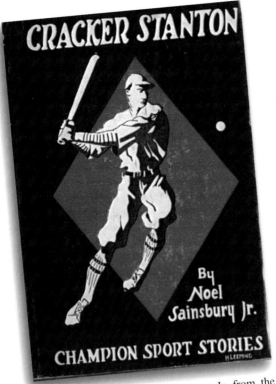

Cracker Stanton by Noel Sainsbury Jr. from the Champion Sport Stories series of eight books from Cupples & Leon, 1934 to 1942.

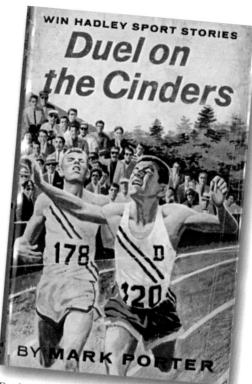

Duel on the Cinders, Volume 6 by Mark Porter from the Win Hadley Sport Stories series of eight books in 1960 by Simon & Schuster. DJ by Mel Bolden.

Sports Stories by Harold M. Sherman

Grosset & Dunlap dust jackets tell us that Harold M. Sherman was from Traverse City, Michigan, and that he excelled in "many branches of sport…during his school days." Sherman's books were promoted by Grosset & Dunlap in an odd way. When the series was printed as Sports Stories there was no reference in the books or on the dust jackets to indicate that they were for young readers. Ads in the backs of the books list detective stories by S.S. Van Dine and Agatha Christie and novels by Peter B. Kyne, Booth Tarkington, Zane Grey, James Oliver Curwood, and Percival B. Wren, which indicates that the Sherman books were meant for adult readers.

When some of the same books are found in the Hot Off the Gridiron series they are coded for eleven- to fifteen-year-olds. The dust jackets of Sherman books from The Goldsmith Publishing Co. say this: "Harold M. Sherman, one of the most popular authors of boys' books needs no introduction to the vast majority of young readers." Some Grosset & Dunlap books by Sherman have a frontispiece by Russell H. Tandy.

Harold M. Sherman Book Formats

Grosset & Dunlap	**Goldsmith Publishing Co.**
Cloth binding; various colors, such as red, gray, orange, and brown	Tan cloth binding
"Thick" books	"Thick" book with poor, but not highly acidic, paper
Plain eps or decorated eps	No illustrations; plain eps
Glossy frontis	Color dj, different for each book
Color dj, different for each volume	

Values for Harold M. Sherman Books

Grosset & Dunlap books	$2.00-$25.00
Goldsmith books	$1.00-$15.00

The Fighting Five Basketball Series

Grosset & Dunlap

Year	Volume
1926	**1. Mayfield's Fighting Five**
1927	**2. Get 'em, Mayfield***
1930	**3. Shoot That Ball!***

*Originally published by D. Appleton and Co.

Rousing Football Stories (Gridiron Stories)

Grosset & Dunlap

Year	Volume
1926	**1. Fight 'em, Big Three**
1926	**2. One Minute to Play**
1927	**3. Touchdown!**
1928	**4. Block That Kick**
1930	**5. Hold That Line!**
1930	**6. Number 44**
1931	**7. Goal to Go!**
1932	**8. Crashing Through!**
1933	**9. Under the Goal Posts** (by Eddie Dooley)
1934	**10. Jimmy Makes the Varsity** (by Jonathan Brooks)

5. DJ.

6. DJ.

7. DJ.

The Home Run Series

Grosset & Dunlap

Year	Volume
1928	1. Bases Full!
1928	2. Hit by Pitcher
1928	3. Safe!
1929	4. Hit and Run!
1930	5. Batter Up!
1932	6. Double Play!

Hockey Series

Grosset & Dunlap

Year	Volume
1929	1. Flashing Steel
1930	2. Flying Heels
1931	3. Flashing Sticks

Sports Stories by Harold M. Sherman

Grosset & Dunlap

(See preceding charts for original publication dates)

1. Batter Up!
2. Double Play!
3. Bases Full!
4. Hit by Pitcher
5. Safe!
6. Hit and Run!
7. Mayfield's Fighting Five
8. Shoot That Ball!
9. Flashing Steel
10. Flying Heels
11. Slashing Sticks
12. Number 44

All American Sport Series

Goldsmith Publishing Co.

Reprints, circa 1940s

1. Captain of the Eleven
2. Interference
3. It's a Pass!
4. Over the Line
5. Under the Basket
6. Down the Ice
7. Strike Him Out
8. The Tennis Terror

Bronc Burnett by Wilfred McCormick

Wilfred McCormick was born in Newland, Indiana, in 1903 but was raised in New Mexico. When he attended the University of Illinois he played baseball and basketball, the basis for his sports stories. He returned to New Mexico in 1930 and made his living by writing short stories for juvenile and western fiction magazines. After serving in the army during World War II he settled in Albuquerque.

McCormick's first juvenile book with a sports theme was published in 1948. This was *The Three-Two Pitch*, the first Bronc Burnett novel. Until his death in 1983 he wrote about fifty more boys' books. There were nineteen Rocky McCune books about baseball, football, and basketball published by David McKay and three more of them featuring Bronc Burnett from Bobbs-Merrrill. For Duell, Sloan and Pearce he did three Roy Rolfe books about sports activities. The twenty-seven Bronc Burnett books that were printed by four publishing firms – G.P. Putnam's Sons, David McKay, Bobbs-Merrill, and Grosset & Dunlap – ended in 1967. These were about baseball, football, and scouting and took place in fictional Sonora, New Mexico. "Cap'n Al" Carter, Bronc's coach, was his inspiration for winning his games.

3. DJ. (Goldsmith)

Bronc Burnett Book Formats

G.P. Putnam's Sons

I. 1948 – 1960
    #1 – #11
    Cloth binding in various colors
    Blank eps; no illustrations
    Color djs, different for each book

David McKay, Publishers

II. 1960 – 1965
    #12 – #23
    Same as in Format I

Bobbs-Merrill Co.

III. 1965 – 1967
     #24 – #27
     Same as in Format I

Grosset & Dunlap

IV. 1950s – circa 1962
    #1 – #15 (perhaps more)
    Tan composition binding
    Blank eps; no illustrations
    Color dj as in Format I

V. Circa 1962 – 1970s
    #1 – #23 (perhaps more)
    Picture cover version of djs
    Blank eps; no illustrations

Bronc Burnett Book Values

Formats I., II., III.	?
Format IV.	$4.00-$40.00
Format V.	
Volumes 1 – 10	$5.00-$40.00
Volumes 11 – 18	$5.00-$50.00
Volume 19 – 20	$7.00-$60.00
Volume 20 – 21	$7.00-$70.00
Volume 22 – 23	$8.00-$80.00

Year	Volume	Publisher
1948	1. The Three-Two Pitch	G.P. Putnam's Sons (#1 – #11)
1948	2. Legion Journey	
1949	3. Fielder's Choice	
1949	4. Flying Tackle	
1950	5. Bases Loaded	
1950	6. Rambling Halfback	
1951	7. Grand-Slam Homer	
1951	8. Quick Kick	
1952	9. Eagle Scout	
1958	10. The Big Ninth	
1960	11. The Last Put-Out	
1960	12. One O'Clock Hitter	David McKay, Pub. (#12 – #23)
1960	13. Stranger in the Backfield	
1961	14. The Bluffer	
1961	15. Man in Motion	
1961	16. Rebel with a Glove	

Year	Volume	Publisher
1962	17. Too Late To Quit	
1963	18. Once a Slugger	
1963	19. Rough Stuff	
1964	20. The Throwing Catcher	
1964	21. The Right-End Option	
1965	22. The Go-Ahead Runner	
1965	23. Seven in Front	
1966	24. Tall at the Plate	Bobbs-Merrill Co. (24 – 27)
1966	25. No Place For Heroes	
1967	26. The Incomplete Pitcher	
1967	27. One Bounce Too Many	

Grosset & Dunlap Sequence of Bronc Burnett Books

1. The Three-Two Pitch
2. Legion Tourney
3. Fielder's Choice
4. Rambling Halfback
5. Eagle Scout
6. Bases Loaded
7. Grand-Slam Homer
8. Flying Tackle
9. Quick Kick
10. The Big Ninth
11. The Last Put-Out
12. One O'Clock Hitter
13. Stranger in the Backfield
14. The Bluffer
15. Man in Motion
16. Too Late to Quit
17. Rebel with a Glove
18. Rough Stuff
19. Once a Slugger
20. The Throwing Catcher
21. The Right-End Option
22. The Go-Ahead Runner
23. Seven in Front

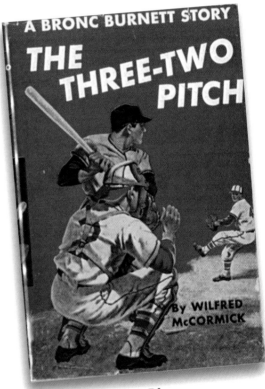

1. DJ.

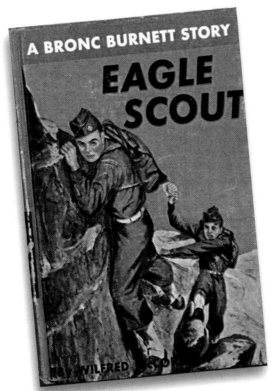

5. DJ.

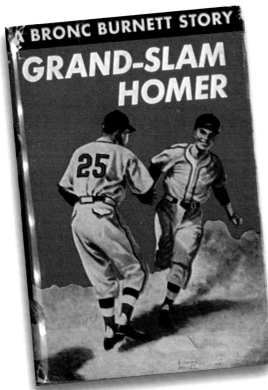

7. DJ.

8. DJ.

Coach Clair Bee.

Clair Bee's Chip Hilton series is probably the finest boys' books about sports ever published. They are also among the best books of all boys' series. Surprisingly, girls also enjoyed the Chip Hilton books.

Coach Clair Bee was born March 2, 1896; he died May 20, 1983. The January 7, 1980, issue of *Sports Illustrated* has a great article about him and his Chip Hilton books, written by admirer Jack McCallum. McCallum tells that when he interviewed Bee in late 1979, the coach seemed very old even for his eighty-three years, but he gathered great information for Chip Hilton fans from him.

Bee set the first eight Chip Hilton books in Valley Falls, West Virginia, near Clarksburg, where he was born, but was careful to keep regionalisms out of the books so that readers would not know just where Chip's high school was located. Some thought it was in Connecticut; others figured that Chip lived in California. In 1941 Bee was coaching the Long Island University (LIU) team, a position he held from 1932 to 1943 and 1946 to 1951. At the National Invitational Basketball Tournament in Madison Square Garden in 1941 LIU was playing Seaton Hall in the semifinals. One of the Seaton Hall players was the great all-around athlete Bob Davies, who impressed Bee greatly. Bob Davies became the model for Chip Hilton and Bee himself was the model for Chip's coach Henry "the Rock" Rockwell. (LIU beat Seaton Hall in 1941 and also won the finals.)

Clair Bee is a member of the Basketball Hall of Fame, as well as the LIU Sports Hall of Fame and the Madison Square Garden Hall of Fame. He was a leading advocate of the three-second rule and he helped the NBA develop the twenty-four-second clock. Bee's teams won ninety-five percent of their games and with him LIU had two undefeated seasons (1936 and 1939) and won two National Invitational Titles (1939 and 1941).

Clair Bee told McCallum that the reason that the Chip Hilton series ended was because the price of the books was rising rapidly in the late 1960s and that television was interfering with sales. Bee also wrote many technical books about sports, most of them dealing with basketball.

Artist Frank Vaughn, who also did most of the Cherry Ames books, executed most of the Chip Hilton dust jacket or picture covers. Vaughn was originally from New Rochelle, New York, and he attended the New York Phoenix School of Design. He did extensive magazine and advertising illustrations as well as other children's book covers. When he was in the Navy he was stationed on the West Coast, from which he also developed an interest in Western themes. His dust jacket for *We Were There at Pearl Harbor* (Grosset & Dunlap, 1957) is especially good and one wonders if the models for the children in the picture could have been his, as he had three of his own. Vaughn's signature is on Volumes 1, 3, 4, 5, 16 and 17 of the Chip Hilton books, and every book except the last one, Volume 23, looks like his work. This one, *Hungry Hurler*, is signed by a name that looks like it is "McDermot."

The Chip Hilton books are known for the high personal values and ideals that Coach Clair Bee espoused. Beginning in 1998 Bee's daughter Cindy and her husband Randy Farley began rewriting, updating and republishing the Chip Hilton books in paperback form. These books still concentrate on Chip's positive influences and his good-sportsmanship, but many collectors are disappointed that the books are now a Christian Series.

Chip Hilton Book Formats

Grosset & Dunlap

I. 1948 – 1950
    #1 – #6
    Bright red composition binding
    Frontis on plain paper
    Decorated eps in color
    Color dj, different for each book

II. 1951 – 1961
    #1 – #19, including first printings of #7 – #19
    Reddish or brownish tweed composition binding
    Frontis on plain paper
    Decorated eps in color
    Color dj, different for each book

III. 1962 – 1966
    #1 – #23, including first printings of #20 – #23
    Picture cover books
    Plain frontis; some have many internal illustrations
    Decorated eps in color; later volumes are black and
        white drawings of sports scenes

Values for Chip Hilton Books

Format I.	$2.00-$15.00
Format II.	
Volumes 1 – 10	$2.00-$12.00
Volumes 11 – 14	$2.00-$25.00
Volumes 15 – 18	$3.00-$45.00
Volume 19	$3.00-$60.00

Format III.	
Volumes 1 – 14	$2.00-$10.00
Volumes 15 – 16	$4.00-$25.00
Volumes 17 – 18	$4.00-#45.00
Volume 19	$4.00-$65.00
Volume 20	$4.00-$75.00
Volume 21	$5.00-$85.00
Volume 22	$5.00-$110.00
Volume 23	$5.00-$500.00

Year	Volume	Pages	
1948	1. Touchdown Pass	212	
1948	2. Championship Ball	210	
1949	3. Strike Three!		212
1949	4. Clutch Hitter!	206	
1950	5. Hoop Crazy	215	
1950	6. Pitchers' Duel	212	
1951	7. A Pass and A Prayer		216
1952	8. Dugout Jinx	210	
1952	9. Freshman Quarterback	212	
1953	10. Backboard Fever	210	
1953	11. Fence Busters	208	
1955	12. Ten Seconds to Play!	213	
1956	13. Fourth Down Showdown	213	
1957	14. Tournament Crisis	214	
1958	15. Hardcourt Upset	181	
1958	16. Pay-Off Pitch	182	
1959	17. No-Hitter	182	
1960	18. Triple-Threat Trouble	182	
1961	19. Backcourt Ace	182	
1962	20. Buzzer Basket	175	
1963	21. Comeback Cagers	170	
1964	22. Home Run Feud	176	
1966	23. Hungry Hurler	184	

1. DJ/PC.

2. DJ/PC.

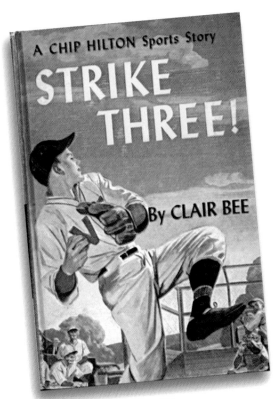

3. DJ/PC.

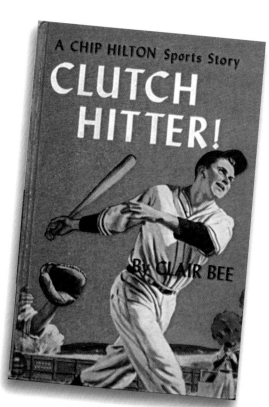

4. DJ/PC.

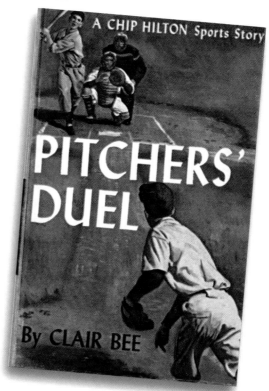

5. DJ/PC.

6. DJ/PC.

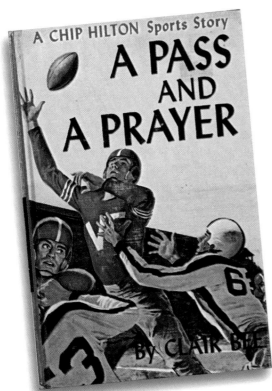

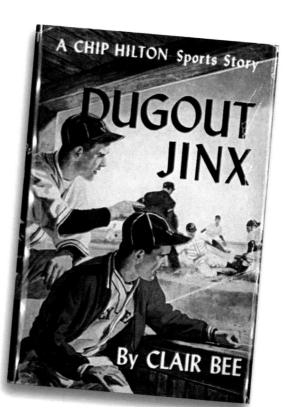

7. DJ/PC.

8. DJ/PC.

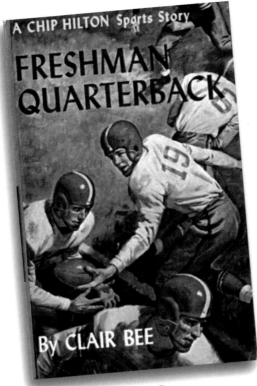

9. DJ/PC.

10. DJ/PC.

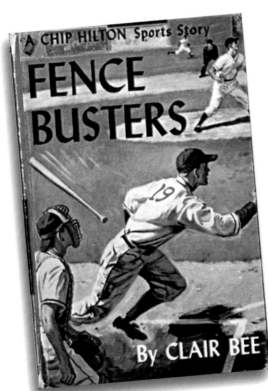

11. DJ/PC.

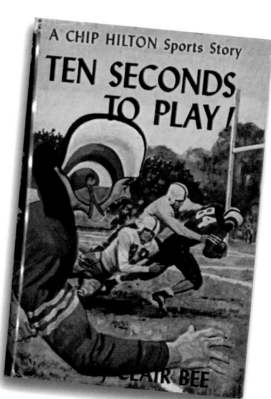

12. DJ/PC.

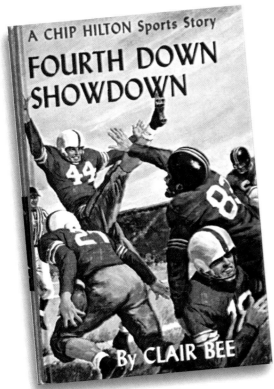

13. DJ/PC.

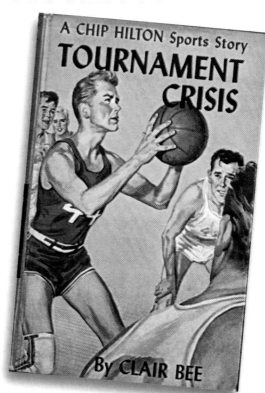

14. DJ/PC.

15. DJ/PC.

16. DJ/PC.

17. DJ/PC.

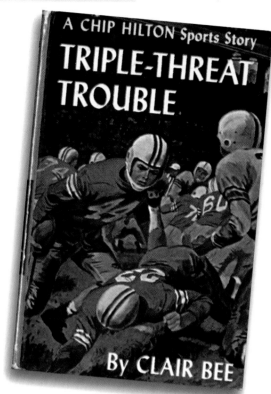

18. DJ/PC.

19. DJ/PC.

20. PC.

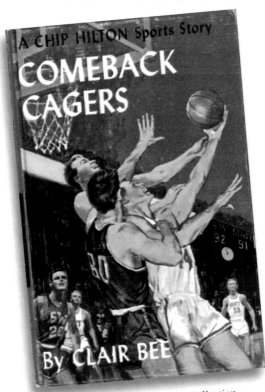

21. PC. *Lorraine Rogers Collection.*

22. PC. *Sharon Kissell Collection.*

23. PC. *Sharon Kissell Collection.*

Chapter 9

The Hardiest Boys of Them All

The Hardy Boys®

The Hardy Boys® books celebrated their Diamond Jubilee in the year 2002. The Hardy Boys® Mystery Stories by Franklin W. Dixon is the first boys' series in which the leading characters began as detectives, rather than drifting into it, as did earlier Stratemeyer heroes such as the Rover Boys. Young people must have liked the concept, as the Hardys have lasted longer than any other set of juvenile series books, with the exception of the Bobbsey Twins books, which were meant for younger readers.

The books have changed vastly since their inception in 1927. Leslie McFarlane, the "ghostwriter" of the early Hardy Boys® books, spoke for all who remembered them when he wrote this in his 1976 autobiography, *Ghost of the Hardy Boys®*:

The House on the Cliff...wasn't merely a streamlined version of the other [story]. It was a different book from beginning to end. ...They've been gutted... Those old books were well written. They had words you could roll around in your mouth and taste. They had funny scenes. They had scenes you could wallow in. ...They had flavor. And now the flavor is all gone. (Page 209)

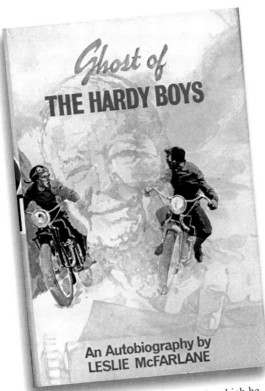

Leslie McFarlane's Autobiography in which he tells of his association with the Stratemeyer Syndicate and the Hardy Boys®. Methuen/Two Continents, 1976.

A great part of my own aversion to the changes in the older Hardy Boys® books and my scorn of the newer, shorter mysteries is that I like things to be the way I remembered them in my youth, a common reaction. However, some of the changes are for the better, such as removing archaic slang and stereotyped descriptions of people of various ethnic groups, and even though the Hardy Boys® books are shorter and less detailed than they were many years ago, the revised mystery tales are still exciting to young readers. Contemporary readers also want to relax with heroes with whom they can identify.

I like the look and feel of the books with wrap-around dust jackets of the Hardy Boys® I first read (the format of the 1950s) much better than the glossy picture cover books of today, or worse yet – the paperback ones. However, then the generation that came before me probably preferred their "thick" red and brown books with the white or yellow spines to the ones of my time. For all of us though, it is reassuring that the adventures of Frank and Joe have lasted for such a long time. Not much else has.

Leslie McFarlane (1902-1977), a writer from northern Ontario, did the first books in the series from Stratemeyer's and later his daughters' outlines. The McFarlane Hardy Boys® books are Volumes 1 (1927) to 16 and 22 to 24 (1945). Many other ghostwriters finished the remaining "classic," or Grosset & Dunlap, titles through Volume 58 in 1979, but the real authors were Syndicate outliners and editors. McFarlane was paid $125 for each early Hardy Boys® book, as well as for his silence as a "ghost." Leslie McFarlane also did the first four Dana Girls books for the Syndicate and worked on the Dave Fearless series, earlier books than the Hardy Boys®. No doubt it was McFarlane who set the "tone" and "style" of the Hardy Boys® books, which other writers followed in all the years since the original edition of *The Tower Treasure*.

Leslie McFarlane, from the dust jacket of his book.

Much has been written about how unfair it was for the Stratemeyer Syndicate to pay low fees for its books and give no credit to the actual author. In the 1920s $125 was about two months wages for a newspaper reporter who had to work even harder and write more words than would be found in a Hardy Boys® book. Stratemeyer ghostwriters were furnished with detailed outlines for each book (more detailed than they wanted to admit), so they did not have to invent the complex plots. Many ghostwriters stayed with the Syndicate for twenty years or more, so the rules must not have been intolerable to them at the time. Producing juvenile series books was a business for the Stratemeyer Syndicate and the names of the "authors" on their books were the "house names" of that "brand" of book. The designers of toothpaste tubes or jumbo jets do not have their names engraved on the products they are paid to develop either.

The Classic Grosset & Dunlap Hardy Boys® Books

The Hardy Boys® books that are most sought by collectors are the hardback ones that were produced by Grosset & Dunlap from 1927 to 1979. In 1979 the Stratemeyer Syndicate took its books to Simon & Schuster (who later bought the Syndicate also). After a nasty court case, Grosset & Dunlap was left with the rights to print the first fifty-eight titles of the Hardy Boys® books, as well as the Nancy Drew® and Bobbsey Twins books Grosset & Dunlap had issued before 1979.

Most Simon & Schuster Hardy Boys® books are short, paperback ones, printed at the rate of about six a year since 1979. This study addresses the fifty-eight "classic" Hardy Boys® books, although there are some collectors who are interested in the post-1979 books. Since even the Classic Hardy Boys® books were printed over a long period of time the entire history of them is too detailed for this book. The author strongly recommends a book that no collector of the Hardy Boys® should be without: *Hardy and Hardy Investigations* by Tony Carpentieri and Paul Mular from SinSine Press, now in its fourth edition. This book even tells how many words were in each Hardy Boys® volume and how many times a character was mentioned in each one!

The Hardy Boys® cover pictures were done by the important children's books illustrators of their time. Among them are Walter S. Rogers, who did covers for

Honey Bunch, the X Bar X Boys and many other series books. A.O. Scott, J. Clemens Gretta and Paul Laune did several books each, as well as covers for other series books. Russell H. Tandy and Bill Gillies, who painted Nancy Drew® dust jackets, did covers in the 1940s and 1950s. Rudi Nappi, another important Nancy Drew® artist, did sixty-three picture cover designs, which is more than half of all Hardy Boys® book covers.

The earliest Hardy Boys® books have thick red bindings. Eventually these were brown bindings, which later became thin gray-tan composition bindings, and then picture cover books in various forms. There are 119 different dust jackets or picture covers for the Hardy Boys® Classic set of fifty-eight volumes. Every one is shown here.

There are four charts that help explain the Hardy Boys® books:

1. **Hardy Boys® Books.** This tells what year each book with a different cover design was first released.

2. **Hardy Boys® Covers.** This shows how the book was available in dust jacket/picture cover combinations.

3. **Hardy Boys® Artists.** Each book title is listed with the names of the artists who executed the one to four covers for it.

4. **Year – Volume – Pages** for each Hardy Boys® title with revisions noted.

Triple Edition.

Triple Edition.

In 1970 the first three Hardy Boys® mysteries in revised editions were bound into a 552-page picture cover book. Rudy Nappi did a special cover for this volume, which shows Frank and Joe in the center and motifs from *The Tower Treasure*, *The House on the Cliff*, and *The Secret of the Old Mill*. This book is very difficult to find in good condition because of the weight of the pages in relation to the simple binding, which is usually cracked badly, but it is only worth about $8 in excellent condition.

Book Club Edition, Type #1

The first three Hardy Boys® books came with revised texts and covers in a dust jacket version that is slightly taller and wider than the normal books. The pictures on these dust jackets are of poor reproduction quality. The composition bindings of these books are dark blue. The first three Nancy Drew® books are also in this format. These books are valued at under $10 if they have perfect dust jackets; otherwise, they have no value.

Book Club Edition, Type #2

In the late 1970s the Atlantic-Richfield [sic] Company had a type of book club through its ARCO gasoline credit card. The first shipment was a free copy of Volume 1 of the Nancy Drew® and Hardy Boys® books.

These were the regular Nancy Drew® and Hardy Boys® picture cover books from that time period, with nothing special designated on them. If one elected to own the "thoroughly enjoyable and educational series of books" from becoming "aware of the current (and quite successful) television series" the next seventeen books were sent and charged to the credit card, followed by the next seventeen books, and then the last nineteen books. This worked for either series, or both, as fifty-four titles were offered in each series. The ARCO credit card was billed $1.98 plus 35 cents postage and handling for each book. (At this time the books cost $2.95 each in stores.)

Book Club Edition, Type #3

These are two books bound together, another format in which Nancy Drew® books are found. The Hardy Boys® books are two books in a mustard-color picture cover binding. The first eighteen Hardy Boys® books were put together two at a time, making a set of nine books. These late 1970s books are not of much interest to collectors and are valued under $10 each if they are in perfect condition.

Foreign Editions of Hardy Boys® Books

The Hardy Boys® books, like other series books, have been printed and distributed in many other countries. The most common volumes are the Collins picture cover editions from Great Britain that have different cover designs than Grosset & Dunlap books and the Armada paperback books from London with another set of cover designs. The most bizarre foreign editions are the ones from Hong Kong. These are taken from Grosset & Dunlap books and look the same as 1970s picture cover editions except that they are extremely thin with a different spine, and there is nothing on them pertaining to Grosset & Dunlap or any copyright information.

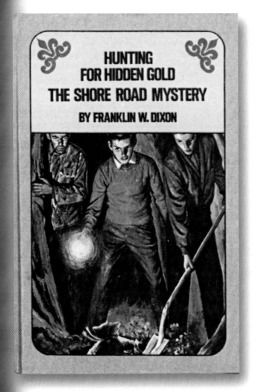

Book Club Edition, Type 3, with two books bound together.

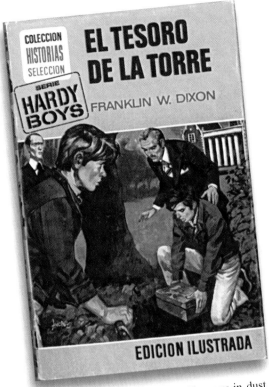

Spanish edition of *The Tower Treasure* in dust jacket; Editorial Bruguera. S.A., 1975.

Collins (London) Number 9 PC, 1970s (?).

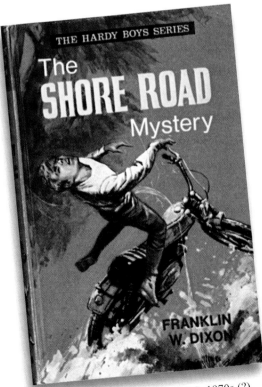

Collins (London) Number 17 PC, 1970s (?).

Armada (London) paperback, 1980s (?).

Collectors of series books also enjoy collecting other memorabilia that pertains to the books. Because of the Hardy Boys® television shows, particularly the ones from the late 1970s with Shaun Cassidy and Parker Stevenson, there are more Hardy Boys® things to collect than from any other set of series books. The Walt Disney "Mickey Mouse Club" Hardy Boys® shows of the late 1950s also yielded collectibles.

There were coloring books and activity books with Rudy Nappi artwork. Grosset & Dunlap put together sets of Hardy Boys® novels, some banded together, others boxed, of the first three to six books in the series. Because of the tremendous popularity of Shaun Cassidy, a recording artist with number one records, there are many, many Hardy Boys® items with his and Parker Stevenson's image. There are lunch boxes, jigsaw puzzles, board games, comic books, toy cars, a radio, a record player, satin pillowcases, and many more, including the best of all – dolls of the Hardy Boys®. These dolls (or "action figures") were made by Kenner in 1978 and are 12 inches tall. They are wonderful likenesses of Cassidy and Stevenson. There are two versions of the Joe Hardy/Shaun Cassidy doll. One has yellow hair and the other has brown hair. The Joe doll has a guitar and the Frank doll has a two-way radio, both of which have a panel for writing "secret messages."

Some of the collectibles have more value than the Hardy Boys® books. The vinyl dolls in particular sell well now, usually for more than $100. (And I can remember when they were remaindered at a discount store for 50 cents each!)

Hardy Boys® Book Formats

Note: The classic Hardy Boys® books involve a complex formatting system. The following is simplified. For more thorough and detailed formatting see *Hardy and Hardy Investigations* by Carpentieri and Mular.

Grosset & Dunlap

I. 1927 – 1932
#1 – #11, including first printings, #1 – #11
Red cloth binding
Glossy frontis; plain eps
Color djs, different for each book; white spine with red shield symbol

II. 1932
#1 – #11
Tan cloth binding
Glossy frontis; brown and white eps by J. Clemens Gretta
Color djs, as in Format I with spine symbol

III. 1932 – 1943
#1 – #22, including first printings, #12 – #22
Tan cloth binding
Glossy frontis, #1 – #5 and #17; plain frontis #16 and #18 – #22
Orange and white eps by Gretta
Color djs; #12 same as in Format I, after #13 yellow spine with heads of Hardy Boys® logo; reprints have yellow spine and logo
After late 1942 the paper is poor "War Paper"

IV. 1944 – 1951
#1 – #30, including first printings, #23 – #30
Tan composition binding; thinner books begin
Earlier printings have glossy frontis; later #13, #14, #17 have no frontis; other later ones have frontis on plain paper
Orange and white Gretta eps
Yellow spine djs through #24; wrap-around djs beginning with #25
Poor "War Paper" until mid-1948

Note: The 1945 printing of #24 (*The Short Wave Mystery*) has a maroon cover and eps. This is very rare.

V. 1952 – 1956
#1 – #36, including first printings, #31 – #36
Tan-gray tweed composition binding
Frontis on plain paper; beginning with #34 also five internals
Orange and white Gretta eps
Wrap djs

VI. 1957 – 1961
#1 – #40, including first printings, #37 – #40
Tan-gray tweed composition binding
Frontis and internals as in Format V
Brown multi-scene eps
Wrap djs, including many reprintings

VII. 1962 – 1987
#1 – #58, including first printings, #41 – #58
Blue spine picture cover
Illustrations as in Format V
Brown multi-scene eps, #1 – #50, 1962 – 1972
Black and white multi-scene eps, #1 – #58,
  1972 – 1979
Crude, double-oval eps, #1 – #58, 1980 – 1987

Note: Since 1987 the picture covers are smooth, shiny stock; the endpapers are blank.

Easton Press

VIII. 1978
#1 – #12, reprints
Leather-bound in slipcases
Reproductions of first art, #1 – #9; second art,
  #10 – #12
Gretta orange and white eps

Applewood Books

IX. 1991+
#1 – #11 (1991-2001)
These are "facsimile" editions of Format I with
  modernized binding techniques.
Glossy frontis
Reproduction of original dj with gold bands at tops
  and bottoms; large Applewood gold seal on front
  of dj on Volumes #1 – #8

Smithmark Publishers

X. 1999
The first three Hardy Boys® volumes bound
  together in one book with a dust jacket. The dj is
  made from poor color copies of the picture cover
  books.

Smithmark edition of the first three Hardy Boys® books.

Values for Hardy Boys® Books
excluding very rare printings

Format I.	$25.00-$300.00; first printings up to $500.00+
Format II.	$25.00-$350.00+
Format III.	$10.00-$200.00+; less for books with War Paper
Format IV.	$8.00-$50.00; less for books with War Paper
Format V.	$5.00-$44.00
Format VI.	$5.00-$45.00
Format VII.	$2.00-$20.00 for books with brown multi eps
	$1.00-$15.00 for books with black and white eps
	$1.00-$6.00 for books with double-oval eps
Format VIII.	The original cost was $28.50. Present value ?
Format IX.	Current retail value
Format X.	$9.98, same as original cost

Hardy Boys® Books

Dates of Cover Designs

1.	2.	3.	4.	Title
1927	1944	1959		1. The Tower Treasure
1927	1945	1959		2. The House on the Cliff
1927	1944	1960		3. The Secret of the Old Mill
1928	1944	1959		4. The Missing Chums
1928	1944	1960		5. Hunting for Hidden Gold
1928	1944	1960	1964	6. The Shore Road Mystery
1929	1944	1960		7. The Secret of the Caves
1929	1944	1960		8. The Mystery of Cabin Island
1930	1944	1960		9. The Great Airport Mystery
1931	1946	1967		10. What Happened at Midnight
1932	1950	1962		11. While the Clock Ticked
1933	1950	1965		12. Footprints Under the Window
1934	1950	1967		13. The Mark on the Door
1935	1950	1962		14. The Hidden Harbor Mystery
1936	1950	1968		15. The Sinister Sign Post
1937	1962			16. A Figure in Hiding
1938	1962	1966		17. The Secret Warning7
1939	1962	1969		18. The Twisted Claw
1940	1962			19. The Disappearing Floor
1941	1962	1970		20. The Mystery of the Flying Express
1942	1962	1967	1970	21. The Clue of the Broken Blade
1943	1962	1971		22. The Flickering Torch Mystery
1944	1962	1970		23. The Melted Coins
1945	1962			24. The Short-Wave Mystery
1946	1969			25. The Secret Panel
1947	1970			26. The Phantom Freighter
1948	1966			27. The Secret of Skull Mountain
1949	1970			28. The Sign of the Crooked Arrow
1950	1968			29. The Secret of the Lost Tunnel
1951	1968			30. The Wailing Siren Mystery
1952	1969			31. The Secret of Wildcat Swamp
1953	1969			32. The Crisscross Shadow
1953	1971			33. The Yellow Feather Mystery
1954	1971			34. The Hooded Hawk Mystery
1955	1972			35. The Clue in the Embers
1956	1972			36. The Secret of Pirates' Hill

1.	2.	3.	4.	Title
1957	1966			37. The Ghost at Skeleton Rock
1959	1973			38. The Mystery at Devil's Paw
1960				39. The Mystery of the Chinese Junk
1961				40. The Mystery of the Desert Giant
1962				41. The Clue of the Screeching Owl
1963				42. The Viking Symbol Mystery
1964				43. The Mystery of the Aztec Warrior
1965				44. The Haunted Fort
1966				45. The Mystery of the Spiral Bridge
1967				46. The Secret Agent on Flight 101
1968				47. Mystery of the Whale Tattoo
1969				48. The Arctic Patrol Mystery
1970				49. The Bombay Boomerang
1971				50. Danger on Vampire Trail
1972				51. The Masked Monkey
1973				52. The Shattered Helmet
1974				53. The Clue of the Hissing Serpent
1975				54. The Mysterious Caravan
1976				55. The Witchmaster's Key
1977				56. The Jungle Pyramid
1978				57. The Firebird Rocket
1979				58. The Sting of the Scorpion
1959	1972	1978		The Hardy Boys' Detective Handbook

Hardy Boys® Cover Types

1.	2.	3.	4.	Title
DJ	DJ	DJ/PC		1. The Tower Treasure
DJ	DJ	DJ/PC		2. The House on the Cliff
DJ	DJ	DJ/PC		3. The Secret of the Old Mill
DJ	DJ	DJ/PC		4. The Missing Chums
DJ	DJ	DJ/PC		5. Hunting for Hidden Gold
DJ	DJ	DJ/PC	PC	6. The Shore Road Mystery
DJ	DJ	DJ/PC		7. The Secret of the Caves
DJ	DJ	DJ/PC		8. The Mystery of Cabin Island
DJ	DJ	DJ/PC		9. The Great Airport Mystery
DJ	DJ/PC	PC		10. What Happened at Midnight
DJ	DJ	PC		11. While the Clock Ticked

1.	2.	3.	4.	Title
DJ	DJ/PC	PC		12. Footprints Under the Window
DJ	DJ/PC	PC		13. The Mark on the Door
DJ	DJ	PC		14. The Hidden Harbor Mystery
DJ	DJ/PC	PC		15. The Sinister Sign Post
DJ	PC			16. A Figure in Hiding
DJ	PC	PC		17. The Secret Warning
DJ	PC	PC		18. The Twisted Claw
DJ	PC			19. The Disappearing Floor
DJ	PC	PC		20. The Mystery of the Flying Express
DJ	PC	PC	PC	21. The Clue of the Broken Blade
DJ	PC	PC		22. The Flickering Torch Mystery
DJ	PC	PC		23. The Melted Coins
DJ	PC			24. The Short-Wave Mystery
DJ/PC	PC			25. The Secret Panel
DJ/PC	PC			26. The Phantom Freighter
DJ/PC	PC			27. The Secret of Skull Mountain
DJ/PC	PC			28. The Sign of the Crooked Arrow
DJ/PC	PC			29. The Secret of the Lost Tunnel
DJ/PC	PC			30. The Wailing Siren Mystery
DJ/PC	PC			31. The Secret of Wildcat Swamp
DJ/PC	PC			32. The Crisscross Shadow
DJ/PC	PC			33. The Yellow Feather Mystery
DJ/PC	PC			34. The Hooded Hawk Mystery
DJ/PC	PC			35. The Clue in the Embers
DJ/PC	PC			36. The Secret of Pirates' Hill
DJ/PC	PC			37. The Ghost at Skeleton Rock
DJ/PC	PC			38. The Mystery at Devil's Paw
DJ/PC				39. The Mystery of the Chinese Junk
DJ/PC				40. The Mystery of the Desert Giant
PC				41. The Clue of the Screeching Owl
PC				42. The Viking Symbol Mystery
PC				43. The Mystery of the Aztec Warrior
PC				44. The Haunted Fort
PC				45. The Mystery of the Spiral Bridge
PC				46. The Secret Agent on Flight 101
PC				47. Mystery of the Whale Tattoo
PC				48. The Arctic Patrol Mystery
PC				49. The Bombay Boomerang
PC				50. Danger on Vampire Trail

1.	2.	3.	4.	Title
PC				51. The Masked Monkey
PC				52. The Shattered Helmet
PC				53. The Clue of the Hissing Serpent
PC				54. The Mysterious Caravan
PC				55. The Witchmaster's Key
PC				56. The Jungle Pyramid
PC				57. The Firebird Rocket
PC				58. The Sting of the Scorpion
DJ/PC	PC	PC		The Hardy Boys' Detective Handbook

Hardy Boys® Artists

1.	2.	3.	4.	Title
Rogers	Scott	Nappi		1. The Tower Treasure
Rogers	Scott	Nappi		2. The House on the Cliff
Rogers	Scott	Nappi		3. The Secret of the Old Mill
Rogers	Scott	Nappi		4. The Missing Chums
Rogers	Stricker	Nappi		5. Hunting for Hidden Gold
Rogers	Scott	Nappi	Nappi	6. The Shore Road Mystery
Rogers	Scott	Nappi		7. The Secret of the Caves
Rogers	Scott	Nappi		8. The Mystery of Cabin Island
Rogers	Stricker	Nappi		9. The Great Airport Mystery
Rogers	?	Nappi		10. What Happened at Midnight
Rogers	Gillies	Nappi		11. While the Clock Ticked
Gretta	Gillies	Nappi		12. Footprints Under the Window
Gretta	Gillies	Nappi		13. The Mark on the Door
Gretta	Gillies	Nappi		14. The Hidden Harbor Mystery
Gretta	Gillies	Nappi		15. The Sinister Sign Post
Gretta	Leone	Nappi		16. A Figure in Hiding
Laune	Leone	Nappi		17. The Secret Warning
Laune	Leone	Nappi		18. The Twisted Claw
Laune	Leone	Nappi		19. The Disappearing Floor
Laune	Leone	Nappi		20. The Mystery of the Flying Express
Laune	Leone	Nappi	Nappi	21. The Clue of the Broken Blade
Laune	Leone	Nappi		22. The Flickering Torch Mystery
Laune	Leone	Nappi		23. The Melted Coins
Tandy	Leone			24. The Short-Wave Mystery
Tandy	Nappi			25. The Secret Panel

1.	2.	3.	4.	Title
Tandy	Nappi			26. The Phantom Freighter
Tandy	Nappi			27. The Secret of Skull Mountain
Tandy	Nappi			28. The Sign of the Crooked Arrow
Tandy	Nappi			29. The Secret of the Lost Tunnel
Gillies	Nappi			30. The Wailing Siren Mystery
Gillies	Nappi			31. The Secret of Wildcat Swamp
Nappi	Nappi			32. The Crisscross Shadow
Nappi	Nappi			33. The Yellow Feather Mystery
Nappi	Nappi			34. The Hooded Hawk Mystery
Nappi	Nappi			35. The Clue in the Embers
Nappi	Nappi			36. The Secret of Pirates' Hill
Nappi	Nappi			37. The Ghost at Skeleton Rock
Nappi	Nappi			38. The Mystery at Devil's Paw
Nappi				39. The Mystery of the Chinese Junk
Nappi				40. The Mystery of the Desert Giant
Nappi				41. The Clue of the Screeching Owl
Nappi				42. The Viking Symbol Mystery
Nappi				43. The Mystery of the Aztec Warrior
Nappi				44. The Haunted Fort
Nappi				45. The Mystery of the Spiral Bridge
Nappi				46. The Secret Agent on Flight 101
Nappi				47. Mystery of the Whale Tattoo
Nappi				48. The Arctic Patrol Mystery
Nappi				49. The Bombay Boomerang
Nappi				50. Danger on Vampire Trail
Nappi				51. The Masked Monkey
Nappi				52. The Shattered Helmet
Nappi				53. The Clue of the Hissing Serpent
Nappi				54. The Mysterious Caravan
Nappi				55. The Witchmaster's Key
Nappi				56. The Jungle Pyramid
Nappi				57. The Firebird Rocket
Nappi				58. The Sting of the Scorpion
Nappi	Nappi			The Hardy Boys' Detective Handbook

Artists:

Walter S. Rogers	Russell H. Tandy	Paul Laune
Stricker	Rudy Nappi	John Leone
A.O. Scott	J. Clemens Gretta	Bill Gillies

Year	Volume	Pages
1927	**1. The Tower Treasure**	214
1959	revision	180
1927	**2. The House on the Cliff**	212
1959	revision	180
1927	**3. The Secret of the Old Mill**	212
1962	revision	174
1928	**4. The Missing Chums**	214
1962	revision	175
1928	**5. Hunting for Hidden Gold**	214
1963	revision	177
1928	**6. The Shore Road Mystery**	212
1964	revision	178
1929	**7. The Secret of the Caves**	210
1964	revision	175
1929	**8. The Mystery of Cabin Island**	214
1966	revision	178
1930	**9. The Great Airport Mystery**	210
1965	revision	175
1931	**10. What Happened at Midnight**	213
1967	revision	173
1932	**11. While the Clock Ticked**	213
1962	revision	174
1933	**12. Footprints Under the Window**	218
1965	revision	177

1. DJ A.

1. DJ B.

1. DJ C/PC.

2. DJ A.

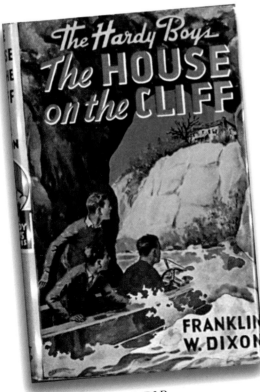

2. DJ B.

2. DJ C/PC.

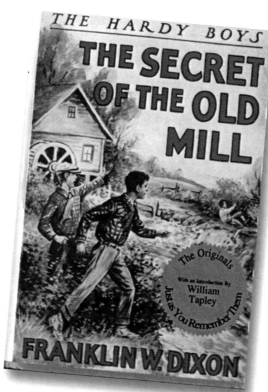

3. DJ A.

3. DJ B.

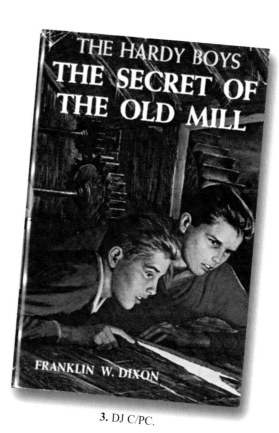

3. DJ C/PC.

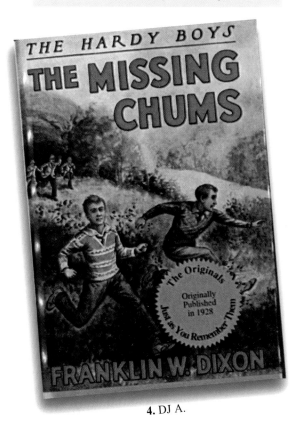

4. DJ A.

4. DJ B.

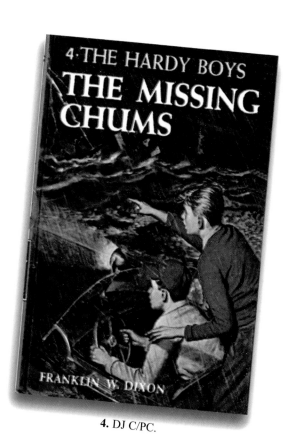

4. DJ C/PC.

5. DJ A.

5. DJ B.

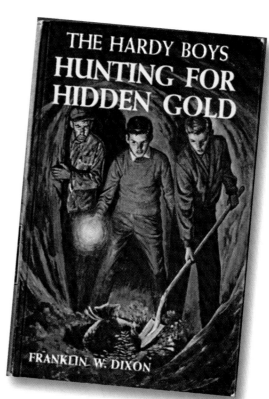

5. DJ C/PC.

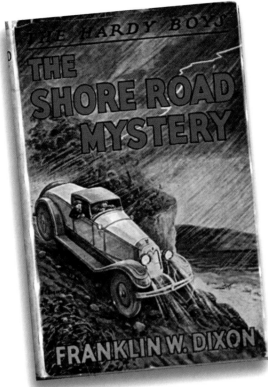

6. DJ A.

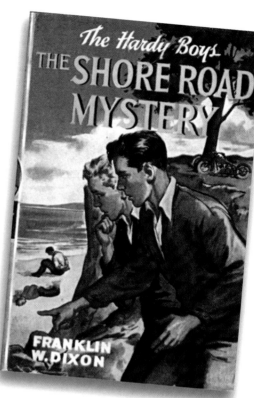

6. DJ B.

6. DJ C/PC A.

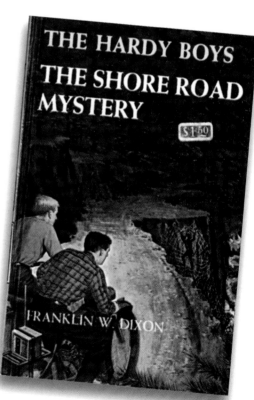

6. PC B.

7. DJ A.

7. DJ B.

7. DJ C/PC.

8. DJ A.

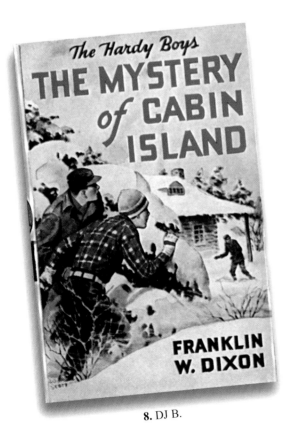

8. DJ B.

8. DJ C/PC.

9. DJ A.

9. DJ B.

9. DJ C/PC.

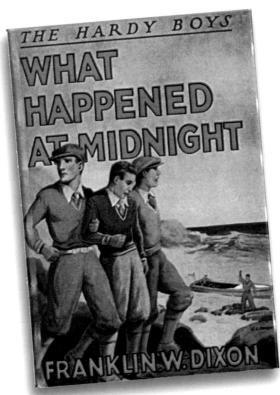

10. DJ A.

10. DJ B/PC A.

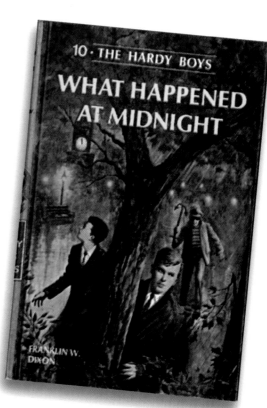

10. PC B.

11. DJ A.

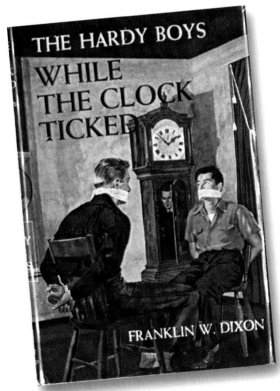

11. DJ B.

11. PC.

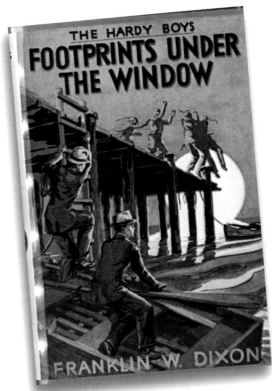

12. DJ A.

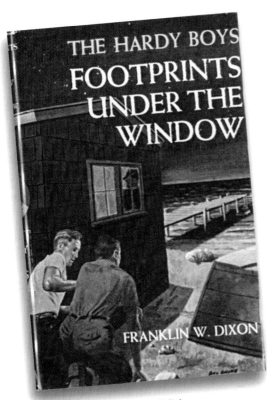

12. DJ B/PC A.

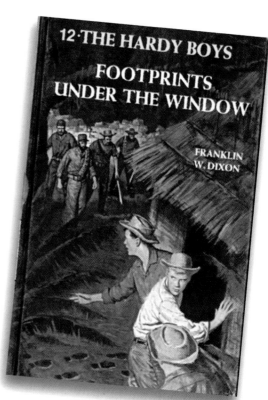

12. PC B.

13. DJ A.

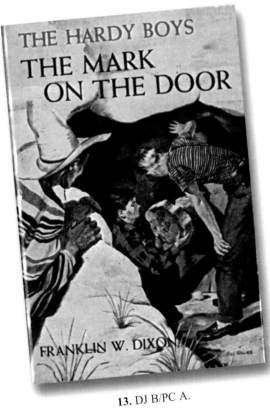

13. DJ B/PC A.

13. PC B.

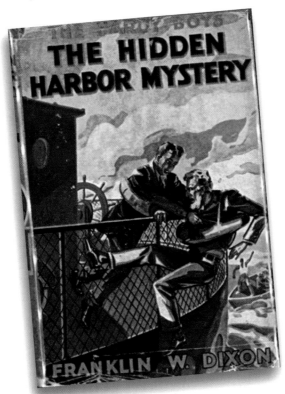

14. DJ A.

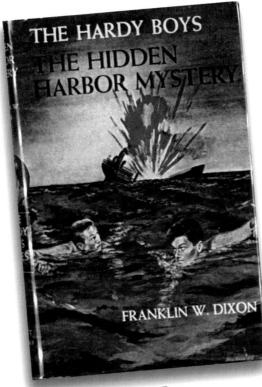

14. DJ B.

14. PC.

15. DJ A.

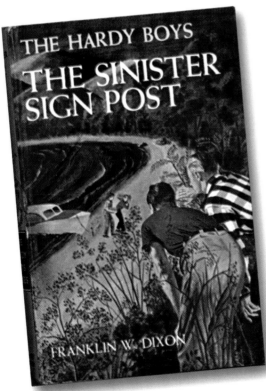

15. DJ B/PC A.

15. PC B.

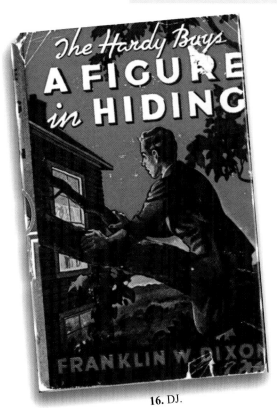

16. DJ.

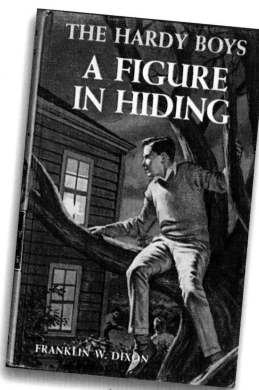

16. PC.

17. DJ A.

17. PC A.

17. PC B.

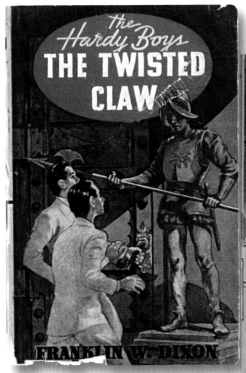

18. DJ.

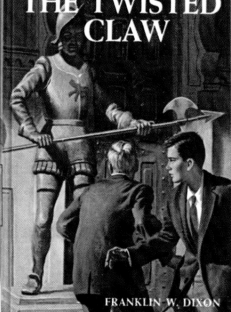

18. PC A.

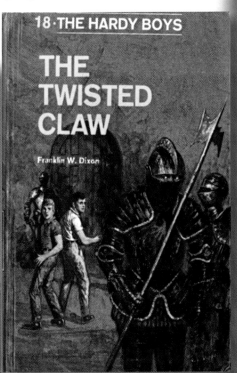

18. PC B.

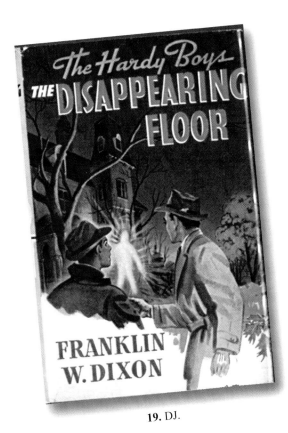

19. DJ.

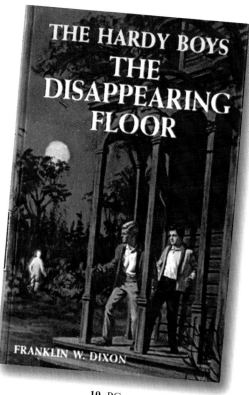

19. PC.

20. DJ.

20. PC A.

20. PC B.

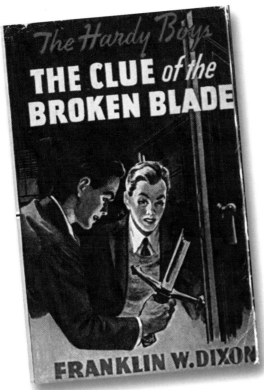

21. DJ.

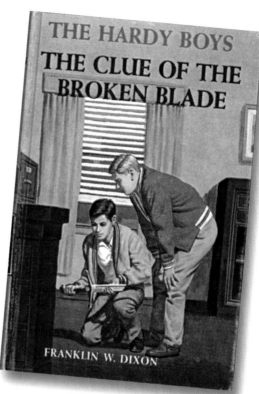

21. PC A.

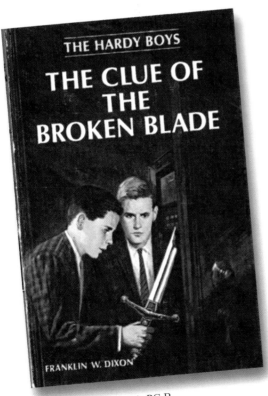

21. PC B.

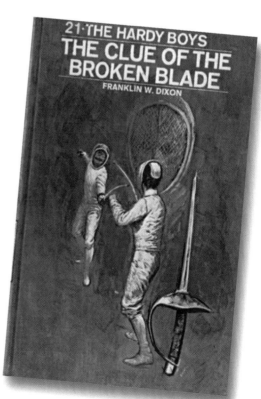

21. PC C.

22. DJ.

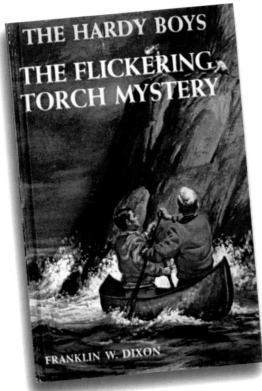

22. PC A.

22. PC B.

23. DJ.

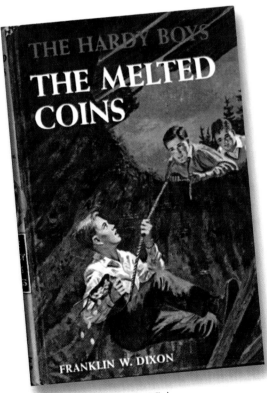

23. PC A.

23. PC B.

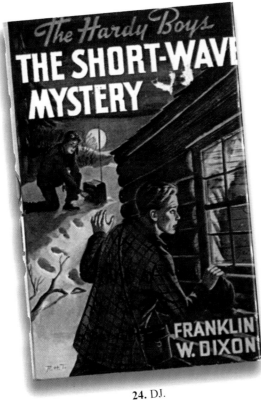

24. DJ.

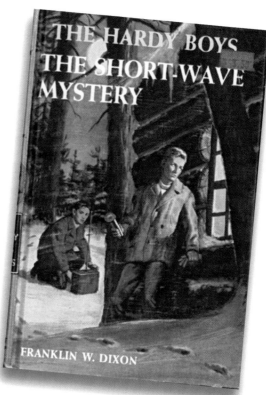

24. PC.

25. DJ/PC A.

25. PC B.

26. DJ/ PC A.

26. PC B.

27. DJ/PC A.

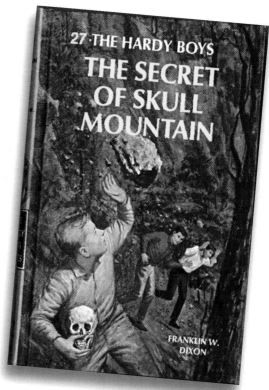

27. PC B.

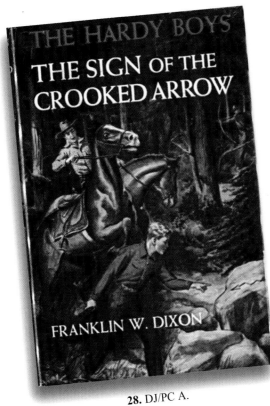

28. DJ/PC A.

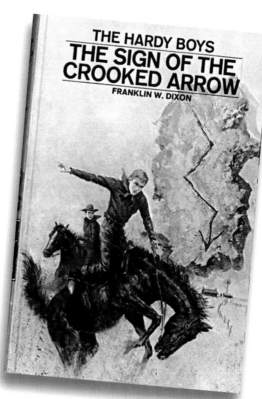

28. PC B.

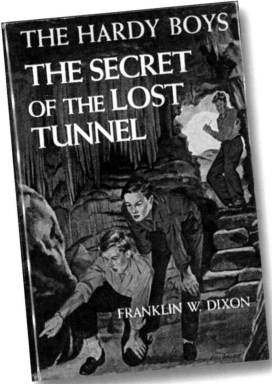

29. DJ/PC A.

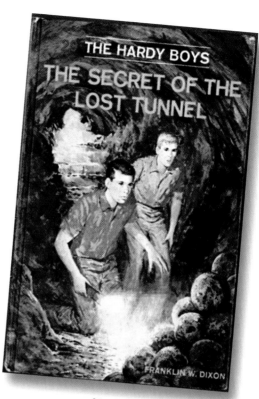

29. PC B.

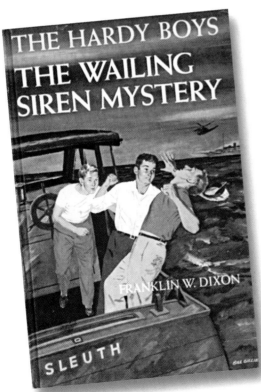

30. DJ/PC A.

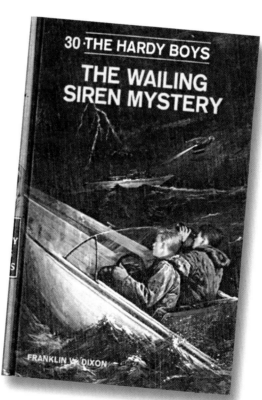

30. PC B.

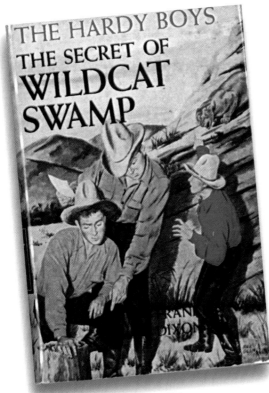

31. DJ/PC A.

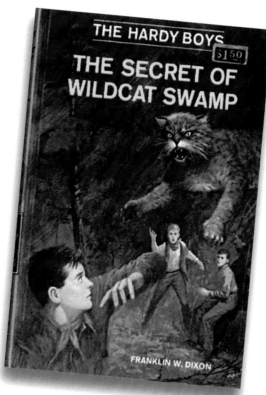

31. PC B.

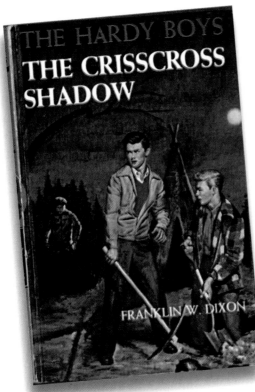

32. DJ/PC A.

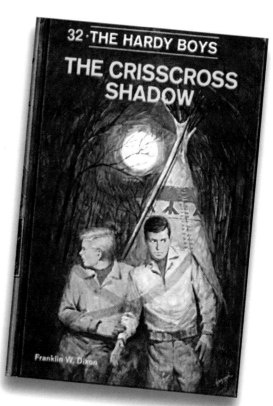

32. PC B.

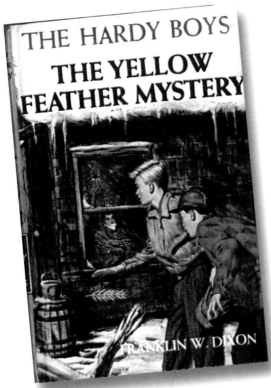

33. DJ/PC A.

33. PC B.

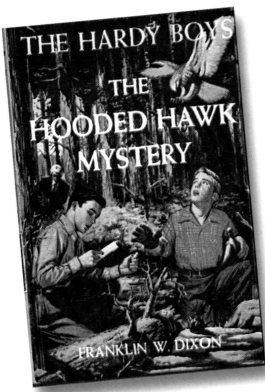

34. DJ/PC A.

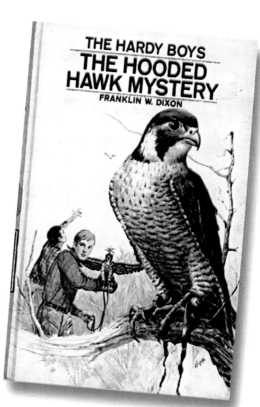

34. PC B.

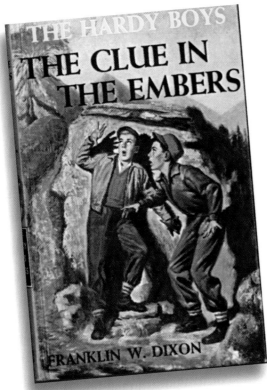

35. DJ/PC A.

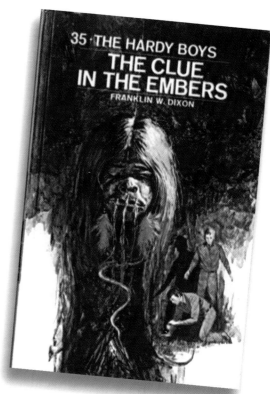

35. DJ B.

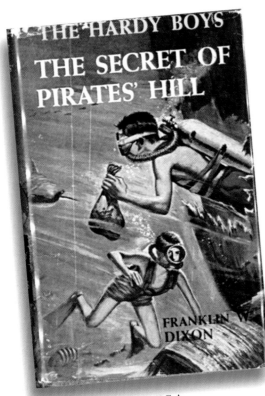

36. DJ/PC A.

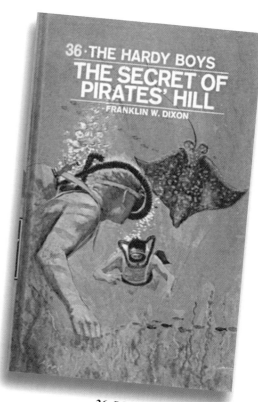

36. PC B.

37. DJ/PC A.

37. PC B.

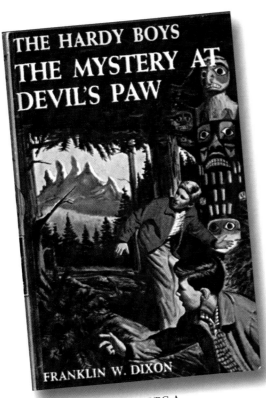

38. DJ/PC A.

38. PC B.

39. DJ/PC.

40. DJ/PC.

41. PC.

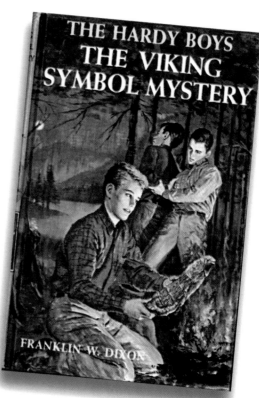

42. PC.

43. PC.

44. PC.

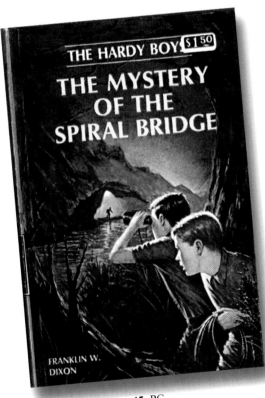

45. PC.

46. PC.

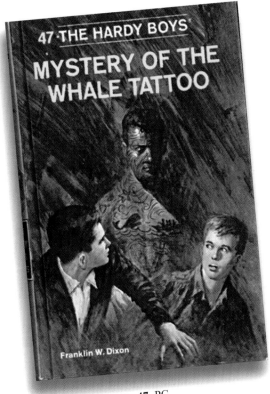

47. PC.

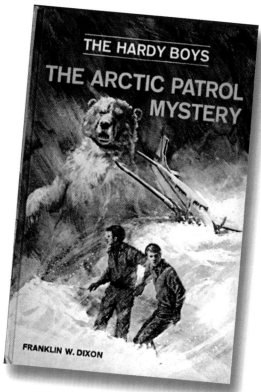

48. PC.

49. PC.

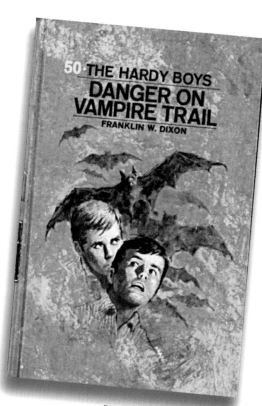

50. PC.

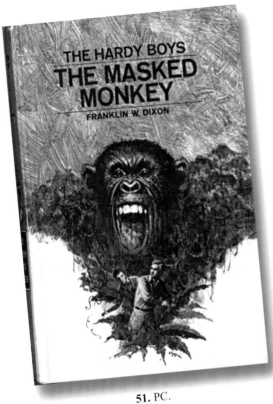

51. PC.

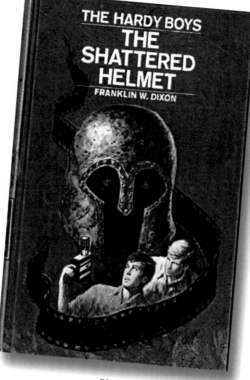

52. PC.

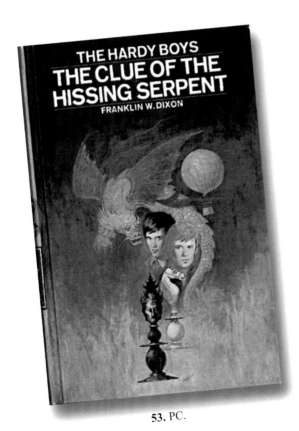

53. PC.

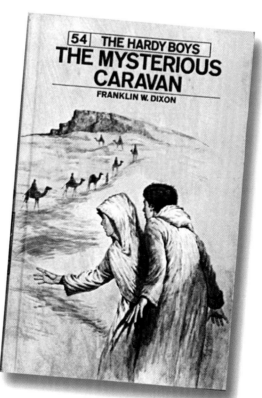

54. PC.

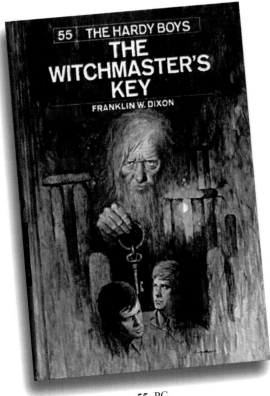

55. PC.

56. PC.

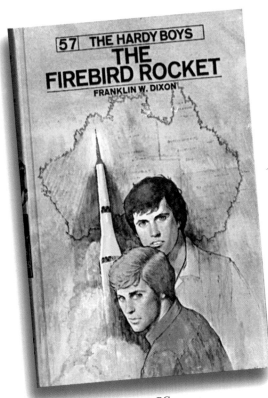

57. PC.

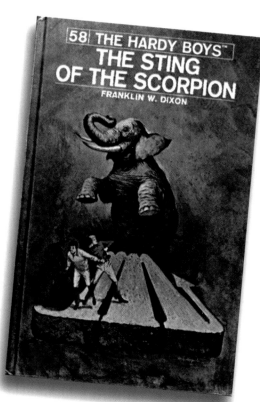

58. PC.

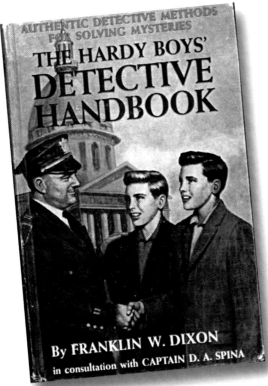

Handbook. DJ/PC A.

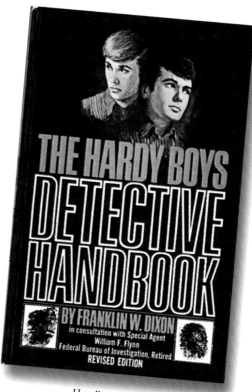

Handbook PC B.

Handbook PC C.

Shaun Cassidy, Parker Stevenson, and Pamela Sue Martin on the cover of the 1979 *Hardy Boys®/Nancy Drew® Mysteries Annual* published by Grandreams Ltd. in England. Shaun Cassidy played Joe Hardy, Parker Stevenson played Frank Hardy, and Pamela Sue Martin played Nancy Drew on the television program in the late 1970s.

Grosset & Dunlap had three other mystery series in development after World War II that gave the Hardy Boys® some competition. All of them were rather successful, although they did not endure after the mid-1960s. Today these three series have many devoted followers. They are A Tom Quest Adventure by Fran Striker, A Ken Holt Mystery by Bruce Campbell (Samuel Epstein) and A Biff Brewster Mystery Adventure by Andy Adams (several ghostwriters).

Tom Quest

Fran Striker, the writer of the Lone Ranger books, authored the Tom Quest series of eight books from 1947 through 1955. The leading character of these books is named Gulliver; Tom Quest is his helper.

These books have a great deal of action and exotic locations, ranging from the American West to Mexico. One oddity in the books is that the final volume, *The Mystery of the Timber Giant*, is taken from Striker's book *Gene Autry and the Redwood Pirates* after the opening pages.

Grosset & Dunlap published the first six books in the Tom Quest series in dust jacket editions. The last two were done under an economical division of Grosset & Dunlap called Clover Books (McLoughlin Brothers), which the company purchased in 1954. These books are picture cover books with a shiny, cellophane-covered cover and they originally sold for 50 cents each. Grosset & Dunlap used the Clover publishing division to extend the life of its other series books that presumably were no longer as profitable as they had been. Examples are Beverly Gray, Honey Bunch and Norman, and Bomba the Jungle Boy.

Tom Quest Adventure Book Formats

Grosset & Dunlap	Clover Books (Grosset & Dunlap)
I. 1947 – 1952 #1 – #6 Dark red bindings; in about 1951 changed to reddish tweed bindings Frontis on plain paper Decorated eps Color djs, different for each book	II. 1955+ #1 – #8, including first printings of #7 and #8 Glossy picture covers The earlier ones have rounded spines and salmon-color eps; later editions are thinner books with flat spines and blank eps Frontis as in Format I

Values for Tom Quest Books

Format I.	$4.00-$40.00
Format II.	
Volumes 1 – 6	$3.00-$15.00
Volumes 7 and 8	$5.00-$30.00

Year	Volume
1947	1. Sign of the Spiral
1947	2. The Telltale Scar
1948	3. The Clue of the Cypress Stump
1949	4. The Secret of Lost Mesa
1950	5. The Hidden Stone Mystery
1952	6. The Secret of Thunder Mountain
1955	7. The Clue of the Inca Luck Piece
1955	8. The Mystery of the Timber Giant

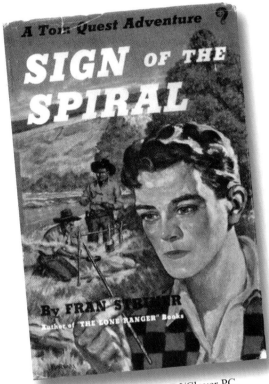

1. Grosset & Dunlap DJ/Clover PC.

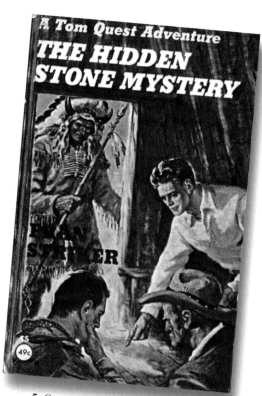

5. Grosset & Dunlap DJ/Clover PC.

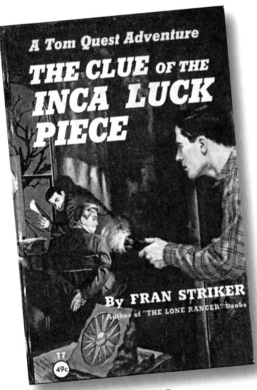

7. Clover PC.

1. DJ/PC.

Ken Holt

Many boys' series book readers and researchers feel that the Ken Holt Mystery Stories are the best written of all. One person, Samuel Epstein, wrote the whole set, with careful editing done by his wife Beryl, which maintained consistency through all twenty-three volumes. Sam Epstein (1909-2000) and Beryl Williams Epstein (1910-1999) married in 1938 and together they produced about 120 books for young people.

Ken Holt is the son of a newspaper correspondent; his best friend Sandy's father owns a small town weekly newspaper. The boys work well together as detectives. The mysteries that Ken and Sandy solve involve such crimes as smuggling and theft, much like those that the Hardy Boys® work on, and the newspapermen fathers provide assistance when needed, much like Fenton Hardy does. Grosset & Dunlap published the Ken Holt Mysteries from 1949 until 1963.

Ken Holt Mystery Book Formats

Grosset & Dunlap

I. 1949 – 1950
#1 – #4
Tan composition binding
Decorated eps; plain frontis
Color dj, different for each volume

II. 1951 – 1963
#1 – #17, including first printings, #5 – #17
Gray textured composition binding
Decorated eps
Plain frontis, #1 – #9; plain frontis and five
  internals, #10 – #17
DJ as in Format I

III. 1962+
#1 – #4, #6, #15, #18, including first printing #18
Orange spine picture cover
EPS and illustrations as in Format II, for
  respective volumes

Values for Ken Holt Books

Format I.	$2.00-$25.00
Format II.	
Volumes 1 – 4	$2.00-$25.00
Volumes 5 – 10	$3.00-$60.00
Volumes 11 – 13	$4.00-$80.00
Volume 14	$5.00-$100.00
Volume 15	$5.00-$140.00
Volume 16	$10.00-$175.00
Volume 17	$10.00-$200.00+
Format III.	
Volumes 1 – 4, 6	$3.00-$20.00
Volume 15	$5.00-$25.00
Volume 18	$20.00-$500.00

Year	Volume
1949	1. The Secret of Skeleton Island
1949	2. The Riddle of the Stone Elephant
1950	3. The Black Thumb Mystery
1950	4. The Clue of the Marked Claw
1951	5. The Clue of the Coiled Cobra
1951	6. The Secret of Hangman's Inn
1952	7. The Mystery of the Iron Box
1953	8. The Clue of the Phantom Car
1954	9. The Mystery of the Galloping Horse
1955	10. The Mystery of the Green Flame
1956	11. The Mystery of the Grinning Tiger
1956	12. The Mystery of the Vanishing Musician
1958	13. The Mystery of the Shattered Glass
1959	14. The Mystery of the Invisible Enemy
1960	15. The Mystery of Gallows Cliff
1961	16. The Clue of the Silver Scorpion
1962	17. The Mystery of the Plumed Serpent
1963	18. The Mystery of the Sultan's Scimitar

Biff Brewster

As the advertisements stated on the Biff Brewster books, they were "adventure—in the four corners of the globe." Biff is a tall sixteen-year-old with blonde hair and he is from a real town – Indianapolis, Indiana. His adventures also take him to actual places, such as Idlewild Airport (now called John F. Kennedy Airport) in New York and Manaus in Brazil. Biff's parents believe that travel is an important part of education so they encourage him to visit many foreign countries. The information about other countries and customs is authentic and well researched. Many different writers did these books, including Peter Harkins, who was the co-writer of the first three Rick Brant books. The Biff Brewster series should have been more successful and enduring than it was, lasting only from 1960 to 1965. There are British and Norwegian versions of this series.

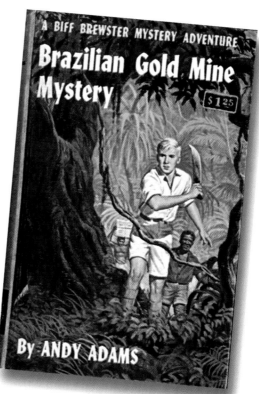

1. **DJ/PC.**

Biff Brewster Mystery Adventure Book Formats

Grosset & Dunlap

I.   1960 – 1963
    #1 – #10
    Gray composition binding
    Green pictorial eps; plain frontis
    Color dj, different for each book

II. 1964 – 1965
    #1 – #3; #11 – #13, including first printings, #11 – #13
    Lilac spine picture cover
    EPS and illustrations as in Format I

Values for Biff Brewster Books

All Formats $1.00-$15.00

Year	Volume
1960	**1. Brazilian Gold Mine Mystery**
1960	**2. Mystery of the Chinese Ring**
1960	**3. Hawaiian Sea Hunt Mystery**
1961	**4. Mystery of the Mexican Treasure**
1961	**5. African Ivory Mystery**
1961	**6. Alaska Ghost Glacier Mystery**
1962	**7. Mystery of the Ambush in India**
1962	**8. Mystery of the Caribbean Pearls**
1963	**9. Egyptian Scarab Mystery**
1963	**10. Mystery of the Tibetan Caravan**
1964	**11. British Spy Ring Mystery**
1964	**12. Mystery of the Arabian Stallion**
1965	**13. Mystery of the Alpine Pass**

2. **DJ/PC.**

Bibliography

Billman, Carol. *The Secret of the Stratemeyer Syndicate*. The Ungar Publishing Company, New York, 1986.

Bishop, Barbara, Compiler and Project Coordinator. *American Boys' Series Books, 1900 – 1980*. University of South Florida Library Associates, Tampa, 1987.

Buscombe, Edward, Editor. *The BFI Companion to the Western*. Atheneum, New York, 1988.

Carpentieri, Tony and Mular, Paul. *Hardy and Hardy Investigations*. SynSine Press, Rheem Valley, California, 1998.

Garis, Roger. *My Father Was Uncle Wiggily*. McGraw-Hill Book Company, New York, 1966.

Hoyt, Edwin P. *Horatio's Boys: The Life and Works of Horatio Alger, Jr.* Chilton Book Company, Radnor, Pennsylvania, 1974.

Mattson, E. Christian and Davis, Thomas B. *A Collectors' Guide to Hardcover Boys' Series Books*. Mad Book Company, Newark, Delaware, 1997.

McFarlane, Leslie. *Ghost of the Hardy Boys®*. Methuen/Two Continents, New York, 1976.

Prager, Arthur. *Rascals at Large, or, The Clue in the Old Nostalgia*. Doubleday & Company, Inc., New York, 1971.

Rothel, David. *Who Was That Masked Man?: The Story of the Lone Ranger*. A.S. Barnes & Company, Inc., New York, 1976, 1981.

Periodicals

Dime Novel Round-Up. J. Randolph Cox, Editor, P.O. Box 226 Dundas, Minnesota 55019. (Old-time dime and nickel novels, popular story papers, series books, and pulp magazines.)

Susabella Passengers and Friends. Garrett K. Lothe, 80 Ocean Pines Lane, Pebble Beach, California 93953. (All children's series books.)

Yellowback Library. Gil O'Gara, P.O. Box 36172, Des Moines, Iowa 50315. (Juvenile series books, dime novels and related literature.)

About the Author

John Axe has written hundreds of research articles and many books about dolls, teddy bears, and other collectibles. He is also an award-winning paper doll artist whose work has been used for Convention Souvenirs, journals, and a series of paper doll books. He is the past editor of *Doll News*, the journal of the United Federation of Doll Clubs, Inc. He is also a designer of teddy bears for Merrythought Limited, England's oldest toy company. John has won industry awards for this work.

For more than fifty years John has read and collected series books. His collection includes every series book he ever had as a child and he has many hundreds of them. This life-long interest has now been recorded in *All About Collecting Boys' Series Books*. Of all series books, John likes best the Hardy Boys®, the Albert Payson Terhune Dog Stories, the Five Little Peppers, the Heidi books and his favorite, the Judy Bolton Mystery Stories. Judy Bolton is the work of Margaret Sutton, whom he considers a great influence on his youth and the interests he developed in life.

Until recently, John was a professor of Spanish and History at Penn State University and Youngstown State University in Ohio. Now he concentrates on boys' and girls' series books.

All About Collecting Boys' Series Books is John Axe's 25th book published by Hobby House Press, Inc. It is a companion volume to *All About Collecting Girls' Series Books*.

Author's Note

Even though I have read and handled many of the books mentioned in this work, it is possible that some inaccuracies have crept into it. I would appreciate any information and/or corrections that may be applied to any possible future editions. Correspondence may be addressed to the author in care of the publisher.